759.18
B
Berger
    Hangin' on

DATE DUE			

81 4468

C L O C Library
Magnolia, Ark.

DISCARD

hangin' on

GORDON SNIDOW
Portrays the Cowboy Heritage
hangin' on

By BRUCE BERGER with photographs by LINDA FRY
FOREWORD by JOHN CONNALLY

NORTHLAND PRESS/FLAGSTAFF, ARIZONA

Frontispiece: *Keith* opaque watercolor 16½ x 34½ inches 1977

Copyright © 1980 Paintings by Gordon Snidow
Copyright © 1980 Text by Bruce Berger
All Rights Reserved
First Edition
ISBN 0-87358-265-9 (paper)
ISBN 0-87358-266-7 (cloth)
ISBN 0-87358-267-5 (limited)
Library of Congress Catalog Card Number 80-83021
Composed and Printed in the United States of America

Contents

Foreword

G̲ORDON SNIDOW has chosen to work in a time-honored tradition but with a contemporary subject — the American cowboy. Despite the changes that ranching and cowboying have gone through over the years, the cowboy remains a vital part of ranch life, and he still works long, hard hours, be it on horseback or otherwise.

A master at catching the character that lies within, Gordon's cowboys are men with weathered, lean faces and bright yellow mackinaws, sitting in a tack room mending a saddle. It is evident that he has sat with them, talking about the things that concern them both — horses, cattle, weather.

My first introduction to Gordon and his work was at the 1975 Cowboy Artists of America show at the Phoenix Art Museum. He has been a member of the CAA since its early days, and says the high point of his life was when he was awarded two of the five gold medals at that show. It was not difficult to see why the man had been honored so well. Since that time, he and I have worked together at both the CAA shows and the Western Heritage Sale in Houston.

Western art is rapidly gaining popularity. More than that, it is being appreciated and understood by people who twenty years ago scorned it. As related in this book, Gordon was one who struggled against that scorn in his early years as an artist. With the persistence of a man who knows his vision is great, he has become a master in the recording of a living legacy — the American cowboy.

JOHN CONNALLY

Beyond
Cowboymania

THE COWBOY WOULD SEEM AN UNLIKELY CANDIDATE FOR LEGEND. IN A LAND WHERE eons of geology stand weathered into view, where plant and animal forms have been more or less fixed since the retreat of the last glaciers, and where man himself has survived for several millennia, the American cowboy has existed a mere century and a half. In the movement of Western conquest, when power was wielded by financiers, robber barons, ranchers, and politicians, the cowboy was no more than an employee, a servant, a hired hand. As great land holdings were carved and consolidated, the cowboy remained a nomad. Material success, normally enshrined by Americans, has forever escaped the cowboy.

Yet financiers, robber barons, and politicians are romanticized, if at all, only as villains. Government surveyors have inspired few dramatic novels. Infrequent are the folk songs about railroad magnates, radio shows about prospectors, or television series about Mormon settlers. The conscripted Chinese who built the railroads have inspired few heroic canvases. Every element that went into the Americanization of the West has been studied, sifted, examined by scholars, caricatured by entertainers, transformed and sold by typewriters, orchestras, sketchbooks, celluloid, videotape, and a full palette. But the limelight has not been evenly fused. The very word *Western*, as genre of book, movie, television show, or even comic book, is no longer slang, and is synonymous with *cowboy*.

I had occasion to discover the breadth of the cowboy's hold on the global imagination when I lived for several years in southern Spain. Andalusians seemed unaware that the ancestors of Texas longhorns once grazed their own hills, but it was the dream of nearly every male through adolescence to follow those cows to Texas and become what he called a *com-bowie.* In small towns the focus of entertainment was the movie palace, which some attended nightly, and perhaps half (certainly the favorite half) of the fare consisted of Westerns, many of them filmed cheaply in Italy or Spain. When "Bonanza" appeared on Sunday night, all else came to a halt. The show's ratings outstripped the bullfights of El Cordobes and the annual soccer playoffs, and in towns where the only television sat enshrined in the only bar, the entire populace — men, women, and children — invaded what was otherwise the lair of the adult male. The most cherished human being, real or fictitious, living or dead, was called *Hone Bye-nay* and was, in fact, John Wayne.

Exporters of Western movies, books, and television shows have found that Spain, as a customer, is about average. A friend of mine knows a Hussar in his late seventies whose land was confiscated by the Russians, who was relocated with his family in a high-rise apartment on the outskirts of Budapest, and whose sole relic of his heritage is his old uniform. To escape the drabness of his life he dresses up — not in his gold braids but as an American cowboy, while his daughter, he notes proudly, sings cowboy songs in a nightclub in Pest. And I have seen flotillas of Japanese businessmen invade a specialty hat store in Aspen, Colorado, and devour literally racks of Stetsons. In the age of Telstar communications and nuclear terror, the cowboy shows no signs of receding as a global obsession.

How could a profession that seems to consist in the tending of other people's cows have attained such transcendence? Images gain power only when they strike mythic resonance, and spring from a realm where even psychologists venture at their own risk. A few factors, however, might be isolated. The cowboy is usually pictured against a far, rugged, clean horizon. The horse he straddles is itself a creature of myth, an accomplice in man's rise to dominance and an extension of himself, obeying the lightning of his command. The cowboy's charges are not pastoral cows — and certainly not *sheep* — but longhorns, half-wild, rebellious, likely to stampede. The remote landscape, the resilient horse, and the dangerous herd come to a focus in the dominant will and intelligence, who is the cowboy.

The imagined cowboy, then, is a man in and above nature. Civilization is reduced to his contact with other cowboys, which remains a working relationship. The cowboy is possessed of skills that are exotic to the layman and that he treats, in his pride, as a matter of course. He has inherited neither wealth nor position, and gained neither power nor stability. He is stoic, unemotional, taciturn, contained: in the current expression, *macho.* His wealth consists in his very ability, his command over his own life, and his freedom to move on. It has been remarked that the cowboy is represented by no single legendary personality, no Ulysses, no Paul Bunyan or John Henry; the cowboy is to that extent anonymous, and *any* cowboy can embody the myth. If he has a contemporary counterpart it would be the long-distance trucker; but the trucker is contaminated with his machine, his chattering CB radio, his unglamorous cargo, while his literal ancestor — the teamster — drove wagons rather than herding cows. Raised to an icon, the cowboy remains, at least for this planet, the natural man.

The cowboy himself, of course, is hardly responsible for such elevation. His aura was developed over many generations, not just by peddlers of commercial sentiment, rodeos, and Wild West shows, but by what has been called the greatest body of art devoted to any American worker — literature that includes the novels of Frank Waters, Wallace Stegner, Vardis Fisher, Walter Van Tilburg Clark, and worldwide best-seller Zane Grey, as well as the creations of such twentieth-century figures as composer Aaron Copland and choreographers Martha Graham and Agnes De Mille. The vision they have drawn on was largely codified by the great nineteenth-century Western painters, particularly Charles M. Russell and Frederic Remington, working in the epic period of the American cowboy between the Civil War and the 1890s.

That cowboy would seem one of the great American inventions, but he in fact culminates a long tradition. His immediate predecessor was the *vaquero,* literally *cowboy* in Spanish, who arrived with the first Spanish land grants in 1598. The first cattle run on American soil were a longhorned variety

4 hangin' on

brought over from Spain by the conquistadores, which became heavier and still longer of horn on our open plains. They were tended by Mexicans and *mestizos* riding small, swift-turning horses and using wrangling techniques that the Spaniards had learned centuries earlier from the Moors and Arabs. The *vaquero*, himself the heir of tradition, herded cattle in the American Southwest for over two hundred years.

By the time Texas won its independence from Mexico in 1836, the herds of both cattle and horses were largely running wild. The job of restoring order to the cattle business was especially dangerous to inexperienced newcomers, many of whom were veterans of defeated Confederate armies and who needed all the help they could get. They adapted the *vaquero's* wrangling techniques down to his very costume — the broad-brimmed hat to ward off the blistering sun; the bandanna to screen the dust pounded up by thousands of hooves and to shield sun-cracked lips; vests to combine warmth and freedom of movement; *chaparreras*, or chaps, for fending off brush and mesquite; and tough pliant boots for intricate riding, the application of spurs and (not least) the discouragement of rattle-snakes. The resultant wrangler was so colorful that he seemed put together for effect, and he fired the imagination of civilized admirers back East and in Europe. The appearance and practice of the cowboy are neither arbitrary nor an American invention, but trace a route of practical necessity leading back through Mexico and Spain to Africa and Arabia.

Once the cattle business was reestablished by immigrant Americans, and particularly after Texas joined the Union in 1845, conditions were set for the emergence of the cowboy as we imagine him. There is an epic sweep to the seasonal events of this period, the spring and fall roundups, and especially the great cattle drives in which herds numbering in the thousands poured like lava through rivers and across plains from the ranges of Texas to the railheads in Kansas. Cattle, driven months at a time, grazing all in their path and raising plumes of dust that stretched to the horizon, were almost a natural force. When it was discovered by chance that steers could survive severe northern winters, ranching spread across the Great Plains to Canada and west to the Pacific, until seventeen states — representing half the American land mass — were largely given over to ranching.

But in a country of so many divergent and explosive new directions, no single endeavor could long prevail. With the introduction of barbed wire in 1874, a fencing material was found that even longhorns would respect, and gradually farms intruded on the open range. The eruption of home-steads and settlements made cattle drives increasingly difficult; then the proliferation of railroads made them unnecessary. By the mid-nineties they had ceased. Smaller, more concentrated operations were increasingly effective, and through the growing U.S. Department of Agriculture and state agri-cultural departments, cattle breeding was improved, care and feeding became more scientific, and diseases were cured. The ranchers who hired the cowboys were frequently graduates of agricultural colleges and members of regional ranching associations. Many more cattle could be raised than in the days when longhorns engulfed the West, and ranching, where it survived, was streamlined, stable, cost-efficient: a business. The days of romance, improvisation, and heroism were over.

It is a tribute to the brevity of that legendary period — and possibly unique in the history of art — that the artists most responsible for its dissemination did so heavy with the knowledge that they were rescuing, in bronze, on paper, and on canvas, the look and feel of a life about to be lost. Frederic Remington, born in Canton, New York, journeyed west at the age of nineteen, rode with cowboy outfits, worked as trail cook and wagon guide, and served with the American cavalry. Charles M. Russell, born in Missouri and hence a Westerner himself, began his career as a wrangler working the night shift, turned out works of art in free time during the day, and only recognized his calling the way that, say, Joseph Conrad realized he was not primarily a sea captain after the publication of his first fiction. "I knew the wild rides and the vacant land were about to vanish forever and the more I considered the subjects, the bigger forever loomed. . . . I tried to record some facts around me," recalled Remington, and Russell made anguished reference to the passing of his treasured way of life.

Both artists, working feverishly in oils, watercolors, sketches, book illustrations, and bronzes, were hugely prolific. Remington, though he died in his forties, left over three thousand pictures.

The titles of their canvases suggest their character. From Russell: *Where Horses Turn Back There's Danger Ahead, Where Fools Build Fires, Tracks Tell Tales That Rivers Make Secrets.* From Remington: *The Fight For The Water Hole, Bringing Home The New Cook, Cattlemen Warning Sheepmen Away From Their Water.* Clearly such art is primarily illustrative, even anecdotal, full of incidents whose generic titles are meant to stand for similar scenes replicated all over the West. Both artists lace their work with humor such as Remington's barroom card party that leaves most of its players dead or wounded on the floor, laconically titled *The Misdeal,* and Russell's series that depicts a bronco bucking his way through a breakfast fire, upsetting pots and pans, throwing off sparks, sending eaters sprawling while the cook grabs his knife — all caught in stages of suspended animation.

Such work seems overwhelmed by storytelling, but both artists were technical virtuosos and hardly innocent of more painterly considerations. Representative is a canvas by Russell called *Jerked Down.* A cowboy, tensing the line on a roped steer, catches the hind leg of another steer by mistake, pulling his horse to the ground. As the cowboy tries to right his mount, a second cowboy prepares to lasso the steer so that the first cowboy can let go, while a third cowboy gallops toward the fracas from a distance. Enough is going on to produce an unseemly clutter in imcompetent hands, but Russell literally pulls his canvas taut by the use of the rope, which holds the roped steer and first cowboy together, trips the other steer, and underlies the action of the second cowboy. Even the distant third cowboy focuses the action in the act of riding toward it. It is the event that still commands attention, but without sophisticated construction its unraveling would be hopeless.

The literalness of Western art, popular with a mass audience from the time of its inception, has fought a contrary battle in critical circles. During the last century and most of this one, American art in general has nursed an inferiority complex in relation to Europe. The first American artists to win continental acclaim, and thus vindication at home, were the European-born landscape painters Albert Bierstadt and Thomas Moran, who extended a tradition that had been launched two centuries earlier in Belgium and Holland, and whose Sierras and Rockies had a safe parallel in the Swiss Alps. But the cowboy as a subject was as unprecedented as, a century later, Andy Warhol's soup cans. Nor was the situation relieved by the growing emphasis on painting as visual music — first the fleeting iridescence of impressionism, then the resolution of subject itself into masses, forms, colors, even absences, so that the subject of painting was painting. If artistic virtue is a matter of juxtaposed sallies of pigment, where does that leave a well-executed stampede?

The public, at least, never disdained storytelling. Since the pioneering work of Remington and Russell, hundreds upon thousands of artists have maintained, extended, and elaborated the Western tradition, a few of them extremely well. But quality blooms in inverse ratio to quantity, and as the West opened to tourism and the cowboy went international, the sunsets grew ruddier, the longhorns more bloodshot, and the cowboy's jaw lengthened like Pinocchio's nose. In the West's great tourist centers, dude ranches, and the National Park circuit — not to mention such art asylums as Wickenburg and Scottsdale in Arizona; Taos and Santa Fe in New Mexico; Jackson, Wyoming; and numberless minor crossroads that function as a kind of asteroid belt of bad art — the cowboy rides herd on canvas. Galleries and souvenir shops, cynically and sincerely, yet feed on a style of life that was fading even as it was caught by its first observers. Critics who have failed to herald the best in Western art have perhaps been blinded by the black velvet. Globally, meanwhile, the cowboy has been Xeroxed by each new medium that technology comes up with — from cheap reproductions and calendars to paperback fiction and comic books to spaghetti Westerns and corporate television, in which artistry and integrity are positive impediments.

It is perhaps the malice of the times, but when a phenomenon is so overtaken by its symbols, one almost assumes that its source is gone, or as marginal as the American bison or the great bald

6 hangin' on

eagle. Elaboration of cowboymania at this point has lost all relation to practicing cowboys and pertains only to a popular tradition extending itself into nostalgia, decadence, and satire. The signs are epidemic — the urban pickups with bumper stickers reading Cowboys (or Cowgirls) Need Love Too or Cowboys Stay on Longer; the six-hundred-dollar boots in swirls of lapis, canary, or emerald, of alligator and eel or traditional rawhide, suitable for wear on Wilshire Boulevard; the jeans designed and executed in France, so true to your form as you do the Texas Stroll at your corner disco. The very movies, exhausted by laconic heroes, tired even of "adult" Westerns, have turned to such parody as *Blazing Saddles*, or such dramatic ironies as *Midnight Cowboy, Urban Cowboy,* and *The Electric Horseman*, while pop singers metamorphose into Rhinestone Cowboys. "If you get an outfit you can be a cowboy too," runs a parody of "Streets of Laredo," and there are so-called saddle clubs where people with outfits can practice roping live steers for five dollars a throw. There is even a post card showing a prostrate cowboy, hat over face and being eaten by vultures, titled "The End of the Trail." Cowboying, having passed in the popular imagination through fantasy and wish fulfillment into decadence, is no longer a calling: it is an act.

Or is it? The historical cowboy never wholly succumbed, and a few artists, working almost in eclipse, have labored to keep the tradition of Russell and Remington not just alive, but faithful to the era. As the open ranges and great drives recede, such painters have necessarily reworked previous themes, relying less on experience than on the study of earlier work, journals, historical documents — and their own imaginations. When one recalls that Renaissance and neoclassical artists reworked themes of Greeks and Romans, who looked back to legendary Titans, one realizes that the historical look is not necessarily a dead end. Many masterful Western works continued to be painted. Through whatever abyss of popular taste, there were still artists who recognized and encouraged what was worthwhile in each other, and patrons willing to pay for the difference.

But the great boom in Western art, like so many other explosions, had to wait for the sixties. With the young breaking into rebellion, the nation torn by a humiliating war, and psychedelics greeted like the next messiah, there was a complementary yearning for a time when values were clear, heroism was possible, good and bad were detectable from each other, and a man alone still counted. And there, imposing order on a herd pounding up dust, giving direction to creatures of brute force, stood the cowboy. Those who could afford it bought the few Russells and Remingtons still available, driving up their value and leaving a hunger for work of similar quality. Painters whose chosen subject just happened to be the cowboy found themselves in what one punning reporter called a "bull market," with their own work appreciating rapidly.

Western art at last gained a capitol in 1965, with the opening of the Cowboy Hall of Fame in Oklahoma City. Sponsored by the seventeen Western states, the Hall borrowed from the finest private collections to display many great Western canvases publicly for the first time. The Hall also encouraged new work by holding annual group shows at which knowledgeable juries presented Heritage Awards in various categories and purchase awards to expand the Hall's own impressive permanent collection. If Western art was rejected by Eastern critics, they now had their own.

Independently but also in 1965, a handful of the best Western artists, seeking some means to establish standards and distance themselves from the deluge of exploiters, met in a bar in Sedona, Arizona, and founded the Cowboy Artists of America. As expressed in their bylaws, their goals were "to perpetuate the memory and culture of the Old West as typified by the late Frederic Remington, Charles Russell and others; to insure authentic representation of the life of the West, as it was and is; to maintain standards of quality in contemporary Western painting and sculpture; to help guide collectors of Western art; to give mutual assistance in the protection of artists' rights; to conduct a trail ride and camp-out in some locality of special interest once a year; and to hold a joint exhibition of the work of active members, once a year." Announcements were placed in *Western Horseman* and other likely magazines, and requests to join poured in from remote studios all over the West. There was no way to admit so many artists and maintain quality, so new members were accepted by invitation only and subjected to a rigorous screening process that allowed only a few each year. An associate membership for the less accomplished was offered at one point, but the public couldn't distinguish between the two categories, the image of the organization suffered, and the idea was dropped. The CAA thus combines the merits of craft guild and club, with the long-awaited trail rides permitting members to get to know each other as characters as well as craftsmen.

The two organizations were, of course, made for each other, and the first CAA show was held at the Cowboy Hall of Fame in October, 1966. It was an instant success, and in subsequent years it was scheduled in the spring so that the show could hang all summer. Each opening was wilder than the last, until patrons and collectors flew in from both coasts, braced for the ribbon to be cut, then stampeded to the pieces of their choice, pulling and tugging over works of art and in some cases actually damaging them, while fence sitters included reporters from *Business Week, Arizona Highways, Newsweek,* and *U.S. News and World Report.* Obviously the event was getting out of hand, so a system was devised whereby the public was allowed to view the works for an hour and a half, during which they could slip an intent-to-purchase agreement into a box by the painting. Then the buyer was selected by lottery — a method so successful it has since been taken up by art sales in various categories throughout the country.

Proof that cowboy art had truly arrived was the birth of a genuine schism. A new organization was proposed, to be called the National Association of Western Artists and to include all CAA artists who had won prizes at the annual shows. Opponents objected that the scheme would cause unnecessary resentment among those left out, and the uproar was sufficient that the Cowboy Hall of Fame, which favored the new organization, unexpectedly canceled the next show for reasons still lost among warring accounts. It was feared the CAA might succumb, but after a year and a half of scrambling, the next show was held in October 1973 at the Phoenix Art Museum. The opening grossed a third of a million dollars, including $40,000 for the museum itself, guaranteeing an enthusiastic host for the future.

The annual show in Phoenix, with its fixed prices and names pulled from a hat, is essentially democratic, and includes the CAA's only official competition. In 1975, three Texas ranchers who are also art collectors launched the Western Heritage Sale in Houston, with the idea of simultaneously promoting good working horses, an American breed of cattle, and a Western form of art. Held annually at the Houston Hilton the last weekend in May, the show is now second in importance only to the CAA show in Phoenix. It features a Friday night art sale and then a Saturday night black-tie dinner for eleven hundred people (roughly three hundred of them millionaires), at which Santa Gertrudis cattle, quarter horses, and works of art are auctioned off. As it turns out, the art outsells the animals. Art grossed $750,000 at the 1979 Houston show, while the subsequent show in Phoenix grossed $870,000.

A less materialist measure of acceptance is that a cross section of American art was recently prepared to tour Europe, and at the last minute the organizers remembered to include some cowboy art. When the show was hung at the Grand Palais in Paris, the cowboy art was given a separate room, was mobbed by enthusiastic Parisians, and turned out to be the show's most popular feature. The flow of Western art to Europe may have begun.

A glance through *Ten Years with the Cowboy Artists of America* (Northland Press, 1976), a survey of work by CAA award artists, shows that most of the members have followed the credo's first dictum: "To perpetuate the memory and culture of the Old West as typified by Frederic Remington, Charles Russell and others." Given the fascination with that luminous epoch, the subject would seem capable of infinite extension and endless marketability. But the cowboys themselves did not all die at the first glimpse of barbed wire. Their descendants may now drive pickups more often than they sit a horse, their chutes may run hydraulically, and their costumes may be corrupted with

8 hangin' on

sunglasses, wristwatches, and goosedown vests. And the cows they punch may be destined for feed-lots. On the other hand, they still round up cattle, pasture them, water them, doctor them, brand them, castrate them, separate them: perform their part in getting protein from the range to the dinner table. Obscured by their romantic forebears and urban counterfeits, they are almost invisible. But it is they, more than the painters of a lost era, who keep the tradition alive. Gritty and ignored, cowboys are still with us.

Gordon Snidow, one of the first members of the CAA and successively its secretary-treasurer, vice-president, twice president, and director, has honored the tradition in a more direct way. Just as Remington and Russell painted the cowboys of their time, rather than looking back, so does Snidow paint the cowboy of his time, and ours. Like his great predecessors, Snidow rides with cow-boys, takes part in their roundups, and values them as friends, mindful that like the cowboy of the open range, the present cowboy too must pass. Some aspects of wrangling — the sun-cracked faces, the unity of horse and rider, the skill in working a herd — are time-resistant, and to that extent Snidow could be painting now or a century back. But his tired-looking men in work shirts and glasses are our contemporaries.

Beyond surfaces, the most crucial difference in Snidow's work is a turning inward. There are no dramatic scenarios involving snarled lines, fallen riders, and broncs bucking through the breakfast fire. When he shows activity, it is of men straightforwardly herding, cutting, repairing fences; or the men are in repose, loafing, staring into the distance, gossiping, enduring weather, waiting for some-thing to happen. In *Vince*, which shows a cowboy posed against a fence carved with the initials of his grandfather, there is a summary of generations in brown wood, brown leather, brown skin, with Vince's singularity summed up by one wind jacket of shining purple. These paintings are less about what a cowboy does than what a cowboy is. They are images, not messages, but if one insisted on meaning, it might be that if it is still possible to be a cowboy, it is still possible to be an individual.

In
from the Cold

WHEN I WAS YOUNG I KNEW JUST WHAT I WANTED TO BE. I SET MY GOALS AS A student and achieved them, set my goals as an artist and surpassed them, set my lifetime goals and am achieving those. Going beyond what I used to think I always wanted, now I just feel lucky, kind of blessed." Leaning back in a kitchen chair in Ruidoso, New Mexico, not a large man but stocky and somehow bearlike with his glinting dark eyes, flared nose, and graying beard, Gordon Snidow chooses his words slowly, with patience, sifting among alternatives for what fits. Perhaps such deliberation is a clue to how he paints, for he has won more awards in more categories than any other member of the Cowboy Artists of America; is swamped with offers, demands, and commissions; and has watched each year's income double the previous year's until he reached "the kind of figure you just don't double." Reflecting on it in his unhurried Oklahoma drawl at the age of forty-three, he makes it sound almost easy. But to achieve fame in a field that has itself been an object of ridicule has taken courage to the point of stubbornness, plus the unexpected.

Two strains run parallel through Gordon's childhood — love of the outdoors and the urge to create art. His maternal great-grandparents moved to Missouri from more genteel traditions in Kentucky, and his grandmother was a talented amateur artist. Gordon sensed her influence through the sensibilities she left his mother. Gordon's father was alternately a house painter and a railroad engineer, and such was his sense of color that if only one wall of a room needed painting he could mix the color to match the other walls of the room — an eye Gordon was happy to inherit. From the begin-

Gordon Snidow

ning, both parents were pleased with their son's artistic ambitions, found instruction where they could, and encouraged him both emotionally and financially.

Gordon cannot remember a time when he didn't draw. As a small child he would copy the comic books, and he can remember hours of lying behind a screen door watching the rain, and drawing a cat that would sit still only for him. He never considered it art — he was just amusing himself. At the age of thirteen he encountered the first teacher who inspired him, and drew a boy going up the steps of a stadium trying to sell popcorn. It was his first original composition, but the teacher was impressed enough to send it to the state fair, where it won a prize. When Gordon was fifteen his father located a private instructor, but after the first lesson Mr. Snidow was asked not to send Gordon again: he was better than the instructor.

Born in Paris, Missouri, Gordon grew up in Tulsa, Oklahoma, where his parents moved when he was still a small child. Every summer they sent him back to his grandparents' farm in Missouri, and it was there that he learned to love ranching and the outdoors as a way of life. The farm was in the heart of Mark Twain country, Hannibal itself was just up the road, and the land and people had hardly changed since then. Along with a swarm of cousins, Gordon went rafting, fished, hunted, plunged into swimming holes, and explored the countryside. He learned to drive horses and wheat wagons in ways that had hardly changed since the time of the pioneers, and he grew up in touch with a living tradition.

In Tulsa, Gordon was president of his class, captain of the basketball team, gregarious, popular, a leader. In his sophomore year of high school his parents moved to Sherman, Texas, and after that to Enid, Oklahoma. As the new kid, Gordon found it harder to make his way. He withdrew, built a shell around himself, and turned increasingly to art for satisfaction. He could draw better than any of his classmates and liked the attention he got from art; but it was a time, he says, when he was really out of character. In Enid he decided to become a Western artist — although all he knew of Western art at that time, and aspired to, were the illustrations of one Harold von Schmidt, which he clipped from magazines. He got almost nothing out of high school, and local instruction was poor,

14 hangin' on

but in Enid he was introduced to oil paint, and his father staked him to the Famous Artist School's correspondence course.

Gordon wanted to be an artist — but he also wanted to be a cowboy. When he was seventeen he spent the summer as a wrangler in Colorado, worked with the cowboys who would later become his subjects, learned their ways, and kept up with the Famous Artist School at night. Briefly artist and cowboy at once, it was a summerlong dream when both of his ambitions came true.

But the moment when the strands of Gordon's life came together in one internal explosion occurred when the Snidows moved back to Tulsa and Gordon stepped for the first time into the Gilcrease Institute of American History and Art. There on the walls, bursting with motion and color, was perhaps the world's foremost collection of Western art, rich with Russells and Remingtons. The very existence of such work came as a revelation to Gordon; these were not illustrations in the manner of Harold von Schmidt, but fine art. He knew immediately what he wanted to do with his life — it was to create paintings like these. He went back several times a week, haunted the museum, practically moved in. How had the artists accomplished it? What were their conceptions, their techniques? The illumination of Gilcrease was the deciding factor, and a glimpse of his own future.

Meanwhile, he needed training. Back in Enid he had gone to the school library to look at college catalogues, found that most colleges offered art as an incidental, and even art majors had to take a majority of courses in other fields. Then by sheer luck he stumbled across something called the Los Angeles Art Center College of Design, offering art every day and all day long. The school had, as it still does, a reputation for toughness and excellence. At that point, eighty-five percent of the applicants failed to get in, but Gordon made it on the first try.

At the Art Center he was artistically a loner. A mere high school graduate, Gordon found that most of the other students had already studied art elsewhere, or had worked as professionals, and their average age was twenty-five. Competition was vicious, and he wound up working from seven in the morning until two in the morning. He failed the English exam by one point and had to take the academic courses he dreaded in addition to art. After two semesters he dropped out long enough to go back to Tulsa and marry his high school sweetheart, Sue, and to earn a little extra money. Sue returned with him to Los Angeles and worked to help support his studies, but he found it took a full semester just to catch up. It was then he decided that if he were going to be an artist, he had to be one full time for the rest of his life.

The prime focus at the Art Center, it turned out, was product design, and students were primed to become art directors of advertising agencies since that's where the money was. Fine art, though marginally offered, was scorned, and besides English, Gordon had to take illustration, layout, and design, though he refused to take lettering. The commercial stress had a reverse effect on many students: those who couldn't keep up with assignments often took up non-objective painting, and the farther they fell behind, the more they turned toward intellectualism. They became the class untouchables, and those who couldn't do decent non-objective work, either, became critics.

If there was anyone still lower than a critic it was someone painting cowboys, but when Gordon returned to Los Angeles he heard there was another Okie just as crazy, and he looked him up. Meeting Joe Beeler was one of the great shocks of his life, for here was someone else pursuing cowboy painting as a fine art. Gordon was relieved to no longer be the only lunatic, but in his isolation he had also expected to be the sole heir to Russell and Remington. It was in any case the beginning of a lifelong friendship, for the Snidows and the Beelers were soon sharing a duplex, and Gordon remembers how years later the Beelers were nearly starving in Miami, Oklahoma, and he and Joe went out and shot squirrels not for sport but for the Beelers' survival.

As a team, Gordon and Joe braved the hostility of students and faculty and enjoyed mutual support. "The Art Center," says Gordon, "was no haven for tender feelings. When they hung student work to criticize, it was crucifixion time, and if they couldn't find anything to attack in the paintings they'd criticize the mats." Once assigned to come up with an idea for selling Philco radios, Gordon brought in a painting of a group of cowboys by the campfire gathered around their little portable and got, he says, shot out of the saddle. The blindness was ironic considering the Art Center's bent toward commercial design, for that was five years before the first Marlboro men sat tough in the saddle with smoke curling over their tattoos — launching one of the historic triumphs in the history of advertising.

Gordon's cowboys may have earned him B's and ridicule, but he was one of the three from his class of eighty-six to graduate, and he was offered a job in Los Angeles by one of his professors. His dream at that time was that a New York agent would offer him commissions to do paintings with Western motifs for some national brand, to be used for magazine ads and billboards. But Gordon and Sue were both repelled by big cities, and after graduation they fled back to Tulsa, where his father was painting houses. Armed with one of the country's most prestigious diplomas, Gordon painted walls by day, wranglers by night, and sold his first paintings to his father's customers.

In 1959, acceptance of Western art reached its lowest ebb, and critics who didn't scorn it outright patronized it for being primitive. Even Western clothing, traditional as it is and now considered classic, was a target for contempt. Those still braving the genre felt a split, being proud of their work and wanting to show it, and at the same time feeling vulnerable and hesitant to invite ridicule. At that point Gordon didn't consider fine art painting a possible career, and he made the rounds of the Tulsa ad agencies. But the caliber of work he couldn't help turning out was better suited for the major Eastern markets, and local employers, finding him overqualified and fearing he would quit, refused to hire him.

So narrowly commercial was Gordon's training, in fact, that he seemed unaware that galleries exist to provide markets for artists, and only discovered otherwise on a trip through Taos. A friend directed him to a gallery that handled George Phippen, then perhaps the best-known cowboy painter, and Gordon walked in with his finest oil. The owner was busy with a customer — then the customer, to Gordon's shock, bought the painting right off him while the owner charged a commission. Gordon thought the arrangement splendid and soon returned with another canvas. A customer again bought it as soon as he walked in, the gallery owner took a cut, and Gordon wound up selling his paintings through the gallery more conventionally for the next four years.

Gordon wanted to be nearer his subject matter, so in 1960 the Snidows moved to Albuquerque and he took a job at Sandia Laboratories. He did technical drawing at first, but was soon put to work designing material to attract mathematicians and engineers for conceptual projects and — what he calls "very schmaltzy-type work" — the annual presentation to Washington that got Sandia funding for its projects. He handled the art for slide shows, designed handmade books, came up with the symbols that sold ideas — and saved his real creativity for off-hours.

It was during this period that Gordon worked out his style. He wanted to move out of Albuquerque; he also wanted to avoid the tight little art colonies of Santa Fe and Taos with their demanding social life and their webs of influence. He bought a huge, historic, crumbling adobe in Belen, slowly restored it, and became an artistic recluse. Two daughters and a son were born. During his spare time, Gordon visited the surrounding ranches for material and, as in Tulsa, he painted cowboys at night and on weekends. He was already making good money through the gallery in Taos but was afraid by giving up the reliability of a job in Albuquerque, he might jeopardize the security of his wife and three children.

It was the formation of the CAA in 1965 that provided the catalyst of change. Suddenly it simply *felt* different to be a Western artist. Requests to join poured in from unexpected quarters all over the West, and practitioners astonished each other with their sheer abundance. The subsequent all-summer show at the Cowboy Hall of Fame was the first dedicated to living rather than deceased Western artists. For the first time, the public witnessed the breadth of contemporary Western art.

Reception was so keen that soon there were galleries and even magazines dedicated to the phenomenon. Those working for years in isolation, like Gordon, suddenly found themselves part of a movement, and Gordon was among the first invited to join the CAA. He switched his allegiance from the Taos gallery to the Cowboy Hall, and allied his reputation with the CAA itself. It was, he said, like coming in out of the cold.

Yet Gordon's first taste of personal freedom awaited the first CAA trail ride in 1966, an experience second only to the revelation of Western art itself in the Gilcrease Institute. The artists and their families gathered in a campground in Jackson, Wyoming, and it rained for days. Most of the families were snug in their Airstream trailers, but the Snidows huddled cold and miserable in a Volkswagen camper. Gordon found himself with twenty-five dollars in his pocket and a thousand miles from home. He had brought his paints along, found some illustration board, scrounged mats, and set out to make small paintings of every subject he could find. He sold them to a local gallery for $365 and moved his family into a motel. It suddenly struck him that with his two hands and his talent he could change his life. But the lesson took awhile to seep in, and for another five years he continued working at Sandia while the ratio between his salary and spare time activity gradually reversed. By 1971, he calculated that working and commuting consumed fifty-six hours a week, and netted a sum roughly equivalent to his taxes. Realizing he had been draining his creativity (and the major source of his income) for a psychological crutch, after twelve years he bid Sandia goodbye.

Gordon is proud to have been the first Western artist of his generation to commit himself entirely to the contemporary cowboy. The subject came naturally since cowboys for him are not some romantic legend, but the reality he grew out of. The very painters he most admired, his three beloved R's — Remington, Russell and Rembrandt — set the example by capturing the people of their own time and locale. It is Gordon's ambition to leave a similar document, so that people looking back when the life of the cowboy has again changed will say, yes, that's the way it was then. Western art, believes Gordon, serves an important function in helping America to hang onto its heritage, and through his fidelity to the contemporary cowboy he hopes to achieve a microcosm of the American West.

By immersing himself in the present, of course, Gordon parts company with most of his colleagues in the CAA. As a partisan, he greatly admires paintings which bring back the days of the open range with new ideas and fresh techniques, and as a reader and traveler he is a student of history. But as an artist he was never tempted. Accuracy of detail is crucial in historical painting, and would require the kind of research he had avoided since school; an otherwise valid painting might be faulted for showing a kind of saddle or gun that hadn't yet been invented. And beyond matters of detail lies a deeper trap. The West was, above all, dirty, and human sweat gathers dust as a magnet collects iron filings — yet too often the subjects of historical paintings are shown in hats without grime or sweat around the hatband, leggings without creases, saddles without wear, shirts without bloodstains, and faces unformed by experience. Such paintings, so technically pure, misrepresent the West as it was lived and felt, and turn into theoretical studies and museum pieces without depth of character.

And here we come to the crux of a Snidow painting. The details have to be valid: the horse anatomically correct, the rope authentically coiled, the saddle true to the region, the steel, leather, and skin scuffed by life. The formal elements of mass and line, color and balance must be so ordered that behind seeming spontaneity stands an interesting, novel, convincing composition. But most important is character itself, that sense of individual humanity so caught in a particular time and circumstance that the viewer peers through the surface into some inner self — a quality that is, finally, mystical. How is it achieved? Gordon knows only that it arises from the deepest part of himself: a gift.

At least twice a year, during spring and fall roundup — and whenever else he can — Gordon travels to working ranches for new material. Sketching is the traditional starting point, but cowboys are too busy to pose and don't care to have artists interfere with their work, so Gordon uses that misunderstood device, the camera. During scenes of action there are often too many things going on at once to remember. A photograph is a good data bank, and from a series of transparencies he might lift a person from one, a horse or a barn or a fence from another, a cholla or mesquite from a third. He might even use the photographic technique of focusing the subject and blurring the distance. But there the resemblance ends.

What distinguishes the finest Snidow paintings, whether of scenes or individual figures, is their sheer ability to sail across the room and into the viewer's attention. A close inspection will reveal that the apparent realism is not achieved with the uniformity of the lens and the acid bath but by the careful application of individual brushstrokes, visually quite distinct, which coalesce from a distance into images of great power. Such art is achieved only very slowly, and learned with great patience. Refined, juxtaposed, distilled until an entire composition falls into forms that are often monumental, the strongest of Snidow paintings attain a presence that is inner and lasting. Like the great art of tradition, it is not the product of manipulation but of creation.

The method serves him well, for he is a major award winner with the CAA, has sold a single painting for as high as $39,000, and has had enough demands made on his person to have become "that poor son of a bitch, a public figure." When did he begin to feel secure? "About last October," he laughs. His easy, expansive manner certainly denies any outward sign of insecurity, and his preferred dress of plaid shirt, jeans, cowboy hat, and grizzled beard, coupled with his profession, even suggest something of the bohemian. But the beard is the result of a contest for a Ruidoso charity (he placed third), and by temperament he is keenly domestic.

One aspect of his career he most appreciates, in fact, is his freedom to remain almost full time with his family. His position as an acclaimed artist puts demands on Sue, but they work together as both business and marriage partners and take pressure in stride. He involves both Sue and the children in his career, grilling them for reactions to his latest work. And the children may follow their father into art, for his oldest daughter Christie now works in a frame shop in Tulsa and hopes to own a gallery, his younger daughter Laurie wishes to become a photographer, and Steve, now four-teen, has artistic abilities he may or may not develop. "I took Steve to a ranch last year and on this year's CAA trail ride," says Gordon, "and he got to wrangle horses, skinny dip, and had the time of his life. The last thing I want to do is push him, but if he does want to become an artist, I wish he'd decide now, when I could help him."

The Snidows have sold their great adobe in Belen and have built a house and studio on several acres outside Ruidoso, New Mexico, which Gordon considers the perfect mix of unspoiled country, town comforts, accessibility to material, and atmosphere for growing up. And while he may avoid art colonies, fellow humanity is important to Gordon. "I enjoy people, like them, can't say no to socializing, and when someone calls we usually say come on over. It goes against our nature not to be hospitable."

"Doesn't that sometimes interfere with your work?" I asked.

"Yes!"

Gordon's achievements with fine art have led ironically to the fulfillment of a discarded dream, for major corporations now come to him with commissions. He doesn't solicit them, but feels that if a company will allow him complete freedom over subject and execution — which is to say, his integrity — there is no reason not to accept, since it is what he would paint anyway. He has never had a commission turned down, and feels confident of selling it elsewhere if one were. But recently a whiskey company offered him $120,000 for six paintings and he refused. "They wanted me to do historical pieces, and that's not what I am. If it had been contemporary I might have considered it. I hung up the phone and said, 'Sue, I can't believe what I just did. . . .'"

In the matter of art's related activities, Gordon has also made his own guidelines. He shuns teaching because he feels he does not have enough lifetime to say what he wants to in paint and cannot afford the distraction. But he feels a tremendous gratitude to the CAA for providing a showcase for Western art that was not available when he began painting, and he has watched the CAA and his own career grow in parallel. He is proud to have been one of five artists who have been leaders of the group, and he has generously served in all of its positions. As an achiever, he carefully selects what he submits to the annual shows, and has been thrilled — even shocked — to win over artists he has admired for years and whose work he has cut out of magazines. But beyond competition he feels gratified to take part in an organization that has welded Western art into a legitimate movement and has ensured that Western art will survive because of its contribution to the historical record and its artistic quality. And the final satisfaction has been to watch younger artists inspired by the older generation, building on previous work until the cumulative effect exerts its influence, in turn, on the future of art.

Gordon's intensity about cowboy art reflects his attitude toward art as a whole. Realism, he believes, is the most satisfying mode for the observer, but any good realistic painting, from a critical standpoint, can be divorced from its content and broken into a valid non-objective painting. The elements of color, form, balance, and the break-up of space work just as well if a painting is hung sideways or upside down. Gordon, in fact, delights in such painterly tricks as taking a square canvas and making it feel vertical or horizontal by skillful arrangement. And like any artist he has his personal repertoire of quirks — the brilliance of yellow rainslickers, diffusions of dust, and especially the bronze radiance of dawns and sundowns in April and October which coincide — providentially — with spring and fall roundup. All the best painters, he believes, are necessarily good non-objective painters, but reality is the most difficult dimension. To capture life itself with a sense of rhythm, counterpoint, and balance is the real achievement.

As for the general public, even during the most arid days of abstract expressionism subject has reigned supreme. People are attracted by content or put off by it. While museum directors denied Western painting even the distinction of folk art, the public honored it with their walls and their wallets. Now even the critics are doing a double take. A painting Gordon did for Coors, and which a Denver art museum refused as a gift, went on to represent American art at the Grand Palais in Paris. And Gordon recently noted, with perhaps more glee than his colleagues, that a Phoenix critic sneered at the annual CAA show for being the usual cowboy art, then went on to praise Snidow's work for glorying in "the false light of Caravaggio." The light, in fact, was a real October dawn, and Gordon remarked that probably the only light the critic knows is the fluorescent tubing in his ivory tower. Still it seemed an achievement that even through a hostile critic, something in the medium had made contact with the tradition at large.

Gordon believes that the popularity of Western art at the Grand Palais indicates we have come full circle. We are far past the point where art has to be European to be good, and America is now reflecting on itself, forming an original culture and exporting it. "We're in the middle of a renaissance we're hardly even aware of. We've achieved an environment without artistic prejudice, allowing a free people to reach its potential, and for the first time we also have a general populace that supports original art in all categories. The great thing for the future is that as we change and evolve, we'll be able to look back, reflect on our national experience, and relive our history." For himself, Gordon feels fortunate to be part of the process, to paint what he likes and have it enjoyed. For the future he sees himself less in competition with his fellow artists, more dedicated to pursuing his own work with greater eloquence. . . .

"But this is getting a little abstract," I said. "What is the actual point at which a scene on a ranch turns into a painting?"

The Source

IN EARLY APRIL THE TREES ARE JUST TOUCHED WITH A GREEN VELVET. ACROSS THE horizon stand ash-colored mesas topped with basalt rimrock like a layer of up-ended pencils, putting a firm cap on the land before it meets the sky. Below them the valley undulates in saffron waves, in straight fences that climb and return in serpentine curves, dividing the dry grass. It is a dryness one can almost taste, of rangelands spiked with cholla of bruised purple, where the most brilliant green is a parasite holly that clings to the mesquite. During the last century, this stretch was a battleground between the American cavalry and Apache and Comanche raiders, but now the most jarring sound is of Herefords lowing to each other when the spirit moves, laying their ears back as if from the strain of breaking the silence. It is a landscape of pale yellows and soft browns, of calm laterals to rest the eye, and a clarity much appreciated by a local observatory. "I come here," remarked Gordon, "with my mind open and my batteries ready to be charged."

For Gordon this, or a place like it, is the beginning of the artistic process. He was here to receive images of new paintings, but it was also a matter of touching base with something elemental, a tradition in which he found great personal meaning and a kind of restoration. We had come to West Texas in time for spring roundup on the 06, a ranch of over two hundred sections, or square miles, sprawled mile-high between Alpine and Fort Davis: if Texas were an upside-down bird, the 06 would be its eye. Gordon also visits ranches in Wyoming, Montana, and New Mexico, but the 06 is perhaps his favorite. Every visit is wholly different from the last, he explained, and I believed him when we saw the high plumes of a grass fire as we approached.

The 06 has, of course, a routine against which the variations are played. Bulls are put out to pasture in the spring and remain with the cows all summer, tended by a skeleton crew that makes sure they have browse and water. In October comes the fall roundup, when extra hands are hired and the yearlings and calves are separated and shipped off. In late winter and spring the cows drop their new calves. In April comes the spring roundup, when calves are branded and yearlings weaned. Then the cattle are returned to pasture, and it all begins again.

The cycle seemed simple, timeless, and potentially monotonous as we drove off pavement down a long dusty road toward the house of our hosts, Joel and Barney Nelson. I knew Joel from Gordon's paintings, was familiar with his tight, lean face and bristling moustache, and knew Gordon's admiration for the ease, the skill and economy with which Joel performs the art of cowboying. Joel is entrusted with a portion of the 06 that supports a thousand head of cattle. The two annual separations, or roundups, are the times Joel looks forward to and relishes, while the rest of the year is spent repairing fences, greasing windmills, plugging stock troughs, doctoring animals, maintaining corrals — all the unlovely chores that make ranching possible.

We reached a solid adobe house with a fenced-in lawn and a stand of pecan trees and were met by Barney alone: Joel was off fighting the grass fire. A friendly, soft-spoken woman who made us immediately at ease, she led us into a house of enormous square rooms, lofty ceilings, and oaken floors. The house, she said, was just short of a century old, and the furniture looked like it had outweathered a dozen fads. Gordon was anxious to catch up on all that had happened since his last visit, so I took a quick prowl through the house. Even the bathroom was as large and square as the rest, with the kind of tub once known as a clawfoot plunge, and a free-standing john flanked by potted plants. Through the windows one caught the flash of a vermilion flycatcher nesting in the yard. Spread over three plaques in the kitchen was the legend: If a man looks out his window and sees another man's house, he is a poor man. By such standards the Nelsons were millionaires.

With Joel and her other guests off fighting the fire, Barney's dinner plans were foiled, so we drove off for a look. There had been no rain since October, and this one was probably started by kids who dispersed from the picnic area to spray their names on the rocks — though sparks from catalytic converters are a newer menace. Fire is good for the ground itself, Barney told us, and the grass will come back with the first rain. But it doesn't help this year's cattle. "And I hate to see the trees go. It takes so long to grow one around here."

We stopped at the house of a woman who had borrowed a large coffee pot from a local church and was making coffee and sandwiches for the fire crew. And we parked by the road and looked up at the burning hill, strung with orange lights as if for a fiesta. It's beautiful, I thought but dared not say, those brilliant flames against the black hills and darkening sky. We sped back to the venison Barney had prepared from a deer she had shot, catching deer and then javelina in the headlights. "I was particularly struck," said Gordon, "by the forms of the dark hills, then the patterns of fire, then another dark hill, with the middle-tone patterns of sky." But the hypnotic flames had consumed nearly twenty square miles, a tenth of the ranch, and if it wasn't out soon we might not only lose roundup, but also the ranch itself.

At dawn we met Joel, who had returned from fire fighting in time for two hours' sleep and was helping Barney cook breakfast. We admired a calendar with a beautiful photograph of working cowboys, and Barney took it down so we could leaf through. The blurbs waxed lyrical about the "myth of the cowboy" and stated there were only a thousand genuine cowboys left. The creator of the calendar, said Barney, had also written a popular book on the subject, much admired by itinerant cowboys. He

was invited to lecture at the local museum and angered his audience by defining *cowboy* so as to exclude most of the cowboys present, including Joel.

The danger of such mythology, Joel explained, is that it glorifies the itinerant who always moves from ranch to ranch and never keeps a job. Kids become purists, expect to work only on horseback, and will suffer no infraction of what they take for cowboy etiquette. As soon as they hit something they don't like — some real or imagined slight, some blow to their illusions such as a ranch that hauls its horses to roundup in a gooseneck trailer instead of driving them on foot — they quit. They haven't heard that the other half of cowboy etiquette is loyalty to the outfit: a cowboy doesn't quit in the middle of a job or speak ill of the ranch that hires him. Historically, in fact, a cowboy might pull a gun on a stranger who insulted the outfit he worked for, even if he secretly despised it himself. And the sad part for the kids is that they make cowboying harder for themselves, for the most prestigious ranches can afford to be choosy about whom they hire, and a quitter gets a bad reputation and finally cannot get a job. As ranches become mechanized, itinerant coyboys are less needed. It is in any case a young man's profession, a tough life, and the pay is lousy. If a cowboy eventually wants to marry and have a family, he will have to settle for a more permanent job, live in one spot, and face the unglamorous responsibilities.

Of course, said Barney, the so-called myth is mainly a problem with town kids, who get their information secondhand. Children who grow up on ranches doing chores have no illusions; it is only the hotshots full of fantasies who can't fix a water tub and will let the cattle die. City kids ultimately can make good ranch hands, but they must face the whole job. Joel, in fact, did train an utter greenhorn from Connecticut a couple of summers back and turned him into a good cowboy prospect, but he started him off cleaning goat pens and only later let him get on a horse to work cattle. It's partly, she thought, that our times encourage people to expect immediate rewards, to reach the good part without getting through the ill, and we turn out kids who are only interested in their hat, their boots, their spurs, and their image, and are really only shadow watchers.

"Shadow watchers?" repeated Gordon with interest.

"Yeah," said Barney, "there was one in North Texas who used to stand with the sun angled just right so he could admire his shadow, and we called him The Shadow Watcher."

Roundup had been postponed because of the fire, but before we could even watch that, Barney had to tend a horse that had a cactus spine in its knee, and Joel had to drive into Alpine to fix a flat on the pickup. This was the sort of luck that always struck around roundup, Barney told us, when Joel was off for days and she had to add his duties to her own. Anything that could went wrong. Goats prolapsed, troughs sprang leaks, the power failed. In addition, it was known that all the men were off working roundup, and was a potential invitation to intruders. The threat had not actually materialized, but once Barney heard a knock on the door and pulled a gun on an injured neighbor who had come for help.

Gordon, Barney, Barney's five-year-old daughter Carla, our photographer Linda, and I all piled into Gordon's GMC wagon and set off for the fire. It was a measure of the ranch's breadth that one had to take the state highway to get from one back road to another, and the ride was filled with further talk about ranching. It was, it seemed, harder and harder to find cowboys with traditional

skills, and paradoxically harder for traditional cowboys to find compatible work. Roundups are increasingly mechanized, and ranches have turned to pickups and even helicopters instead of horses. On many spreads cattle are used to being fed every day from the back of a pickup, so the very sight of a truck becomes a lure when it is time to round them up. The 06 cowboys shoe their own horses, but the ranch does take advantage of a program at Sul Ross State University in Alpine, whereby students shoe the ranch's hundred-odd horses in return for the practice. Many cowboys now work primarily at gas stations, feed stores, and the like in towns like Alpine and only hire out on weekends. Automation has struck even the cowboy, it seems, and traditional ranching is being diluted, or dying out.

Yet on some spreads, like the 06, the terrain is simply too rugged for wholly mechanized operations, and men on horseback are still the most efficient way of herding beef. It might take twenty men to perform daily operations that four can now handle with machines, even on the 06, but the traditional roundup is a matter of utility, not just nostalgia. Already the 06 has found it practical to reintroduce two horse-drawn wagons to put out feed, and perhaps the fuel shortage will heighten that trend until there will again be cattle drives to the nearest railroad. Joel, for one, thinks that a possibility. Of course, he says, they will need a more serious crop of cowboys. . . .

"By the way, are you going to paint The Shadow Watcher?" I asked Gordon.

He laughed. "I've already got it worked out in my head. Cowboys always see themselves on horseback, so I'll have to have him mounted, and I'll bring the shadow right up to him by having him ride past a cutbank or something close."

We drove down a long valley toward Headquarters, a large and thickly shaded ranch house the Kokernot family moved into when they consolidated the ranch in 1906. Beyond it we climbed toward a mountainous, boulder-infested area of the ranch called the Arkansas, where they pastured the horses or, as they said, sent them to rock school. We wound across a long straw-colored mesa, and Gordon said it was hard to believe these were the same hills that turned a felt green during fall roundup after the September rains. Suddenly the land dropped away, and the scene before us looked

hangin' on 27

like the aftermath of a volcanic eruption. Entire hillsides seethed like freshly cooled lava, smoking and black, pocked with icy blue where a sotol, a large agave, had burned more slowly into a pool of ash. "All the pretty trees are all naked," said Carla.

The road ahead curved in pale tracks through black tundra, toward an isolated patch still burning. We continued on foot. Reaching the flames we could feel the scorch on our faces, while the sky beyond trembled as if through wet glass. The fire advanced in a steady line, a black landscape consuming a blond one in a brilliant orange band, so slowly it seemed stationary, then leapt five feet at once in a breath of wind. The air smelled thin and sweetly metallic, while the fire crackled in a continual rush of oxygen within which lay something terrifyingly still. On the walk back to the truck, we saw a flock of horned larks feeding over the scorched ground, then came to a group of cows stranded in a small unburned patch with a salt lick, a watertank, and nothing more to eat. How impassively, I thought, life continues or gives in.

As we drove back to Headquarters, grateful at least that the fire had exhausted itself, four cowboys came galloping toward us. I had seen what I took for cowboys all my life, but after so much talk these were newly colorful, exotic, unexpected. When we bailed out of the truck, Gordon beamed expansively and introduced us all around: these were his people. "A little refreshment?" he asked. It used to be a point of honor among certain cowboys never to appear weak enough to take a drink during the day, but these were all enthusiasm when he reached into the cooler for the Dr. Pepper and Mountain Dew. "Well, Mark," said Gordon to the youngest of the four, "any hair on your upper lip yet?"

With candid blue eyes and brown locks curling from his broad-brimmed hat, Mark flashed a dazzling white smile and was about to speak when another cowboy broke in. "He's tryin' to grow a moustache, but when he's asleep we sprinkle milk on his lips and the cat keeps lickin' it off."

I realized at once who Mark was, for Gordon had told the story of a kid from a broken home who had arrived two years ago at the o6 in his hand-me-down clothes, emaciated and trembling, almost unable to speak. He knew nothing about ranches, could not even sit a horse, and he simply thrust himself upon them wanting to be a cowboy. He was, they said, like a whipped dog: wouldn't eat, wouldn't look anyone in the eye, wouldn't even get out of bed in the morning. But because he so genuinely wanted to be part of the ranch they put up with him. Once he could ride a horse he would get in front of the cattle, or crowd them, unable to anticipate their movements, and he got in the way of the other cowboys doing their job. The cowboys responded by yelling at him, treating him rough, teasing him unmercifully — it was their way of showing him affection and turning him into a cowboy. Mark did as he was told, picked up cowboying quickly, and as he became an accomplished rider, roper, and part of the group, his self-confidence bloomed. The foreman fathered him, the cook called him "mah son," and the Mexicans called him *ojos azules*, or blue eyes. It was hard to believe he hadn't always been so outgoing, humorous, and ready for whatever came next. If cowboying was the demise of town kids looking for a romantic image, Mark was the reverse — a kid who faced the life completely and discovered himself.

But we were wrong, it seemed, about the fire dying out; it had broken anew further on and the cowboys were on their way. We turned the truck around, passed the burned area we had already inspected and rounded the shoulder of the next hill. Suddenly the desolation gave way to a spectacle of fire, humanity, and smoke. The entire mesa above us seemed to be steaming from the inside, with a line of flames curling upward toward rimrock while another fire burned toward us from the canyon below. Smoke boiled uphill like a blue surf. Scattered along the road were assorted pickups, cars, and a fire truck from a local fire department. Several dozen people were beating back the upper fire while the volunteer department prepared to halt the lower one by backfiring, a controlled burning of grass just below us that would deprive the fire of fuel. Chris Lacy, the young manager of the o6 and grandson of the retired owners, the Kokernots, was supervising while his wife Diane handed out brooms

and wet burlap bags, or tow sacks, from the back of the pickup. Our arrival was greeted with enthusiasm and a tow sack for each of us.

As novice firefighters we were assigned to the end of the line to make sure fire didn't break out anew where it had already been checked. At the head of the line, men with shovels and brooms scraped a small clearing, while those behind struck the flames inside with successive whaps of burlap. The entire operation crawled from windward to leeward, climbing slowly toward rimrock and erasing fire behind it. Those of us behind had to keep a sharp eye on the yucca and soapweed, smouldering concentrations awaiting a breath of wind to launch new flames across the clearing. Wherever fire broke out fresh we gathered lunging and striking as if beating back snakes, and I was impressed with the power of wet burlap. The sustained heat stung like a bad sunburn, while sudden shifts of smoke sent us scurrying downhill with seized lungs and stinging eyes. Once I saw a ground squirrel in the burned area, squealing frantically from rock to rock. Just when I was congratulating myself on learning the ways of fire, a sudden gust fired some high grass and I barely leapt back in time.

Throughout the afternoon I was struck by the social democracy of the line, which found the Lacys working side by side with cowboys, town volunteers, and "wets," the hired Mexicans, to

30 hangin'on

which we added an artist, a writer, and a photographer. Mark kept riding between the fire line and the trucks, running errands and advancing vehicles, assuring us that yesterday he had put in a full shift at the flames. Once Gordon seemed to be studying something downhill, as if sizing it up, then announced, "Watching the hot spot."

"What?" I said, then caught Joel standing with a tow sack in front of a smouldering soapweed. "Oh," I said, recognizing in his slow diction the title of a future painting — *Watching the Hot Spot.*

We fought the fire two-thirds of the way to rimrock, then somebody yelled it had broken back out below, and we returned to begin it all again. This is hopeless, I thought, all it takes is one spark in one gust to unravel it all. "When does the wind stop around here?" I asked Barney.

"About when we need it to run the windmills."

We fought the smoke and the heat the rest of the day, people clustered at intervals all over the hillside, and this time we battled it all the way to rimrock. The line seemed to hold. All but the cowboys returned toward the other fire in the canyon. We repaired to the back of Gordon's truck, which was turning into a rolling cantina. Gordon had deliberately brought more than we could possibly drink so that he could offer it to the cowboys, and I could see that beyond the camaraderie it was a means of drawing the cowboys out, of making them available for study. When Mark dismounted to get his Seven Up, one of the other cowboys loosened his saddle and unbridled his horse. There commenced a minor rodeo in which the other cowboys roped Mark's horse and Mark tried to spook the mounts of his attackers. Gordon said that such horseplay would never happen with a boss around, since it is a likely source of accident, but after the tensions of fire fighting it seemed almost like reasonable behavior.

We drove back to the canyon where the volunteer fire department was backfiring against the lower fire. As we approached in the late sun, curtains of smoke rose in opalescent billows from sulphur to turquoise, while before them spread a black frieze of cowboys, horses, and trucks. We emptied rolls of film on the scene, and remained until nightfall. Both fires now seemed to be con-

32 hangin' on

tained, and when we caught a last look from below, pockets of flame still flared like a hilltop city, orange and dancing.

News came in the morning that the embers had died in the night, this time more convincingly, and the danger seemed over. Roundup would begin late afternoon, but meanwhile all hands were exhausted from fire fighting, and the day was reserved for recovery. I too was glad for a few tranquil hours, and more thoroughly browsed the Nelson household. The bookcase was filled with works about ranching and the West, supplemented with the Harvard Classics and a generous smattering of contemporary American novels. On the coffee table lay magazines with articles about Gordon, as well as copies of *Western Horseman* and other magazines with pieces about horses and ranching by Barney. Besides running the household, raising a daughter, helping Joel with his chores, and her new career of photojournalism, Barney also works full time as a secretary at Sul Ross State University in Alpine. Barney and Joel both have college degrees and have deliberately chosen ranch life over a number of simpler alternatives. "Because this area is so isolated and the life so physical, outsiders have misconceptions about those who live here," said Joel at one point. "When you write about us, please let people know we're not hicks."

Early afternoon we headed to the house of Jack Pharriss, foreman of the 06 and the subject of *Saturday Night Whiskey, A Bunch of Sunday Morning Hurt*, a canvas showing Pharriss squinting at dawn in that false light of Caravaggio the Phoenix critic had so admired, and which had won Best of Show in the CAA exhibition in 1978. A road crew was oiling the drive to Pharriss's house, and as we passed, Gordon said, "See that guy on the paving machine? He's the cowboy in *Looking for the Old Piebald Mare.*" Clearly we were deep into Snidow country.

Jack was as rugged and compact as the painting suggested, and with him was a younger cowboy named Steve, with black hair and a dark, classically chiseled face. Jack offered us coffee and Steve said,

"You're gettin' pretty famous, Gordon. I see either your face or your pictures in half the magazines."

"Would you like to see a few new ones?" asked Gordon. He went to the truck for a box of slides of his paintings, and the cowboys held them to the window.

"Oh, there's the roan that escaped with the loose saddle and wound up lame," said Jack.

"And there's the Mexican who took off in such a hurry for Wyoming," said Steve. "Wonder if he'll show up around here again." Reduced to transparencies the paintings lost much of their subtlety, and the cowboys held them in quick succession to the light, gossiping about the subjects. Finally Steve said, "These paintin's sure look a lot like photographs. Is that what you were aimin' at?"

Gordon hesitated, then said, "Well, it's realism."

After coffee the cowboys accompanied us to the truck. "Got something else for you," Gordon said, and pulled out a tube of posters of *Saturday Night Whiskey,* which had been used to announce the 1979 CAA show in Phoenix. He and Jack autographed them on the hood of the truck, the painter signing the right shoulder, the subject signing the left, then Gordon gave Jack several to give to family and friends, and one each to Linda and myself.

As we drove away, Gordon said, "It really pleases me that they relate to the things they know in the paintings and find they look right. That's as important to me as the critics going on about line and space."

"Steve would certainly make a good subject," I said. "Have you ever painted him?"

"That's an odd thing. Whenever I take out the camera he looks the other way, gets his hand over his face or somehow makes it impossible to get his picture. I've told him I'll never paint him if he doesn't want me to, but still he hides. Seems he's part Indian and believes that if his picture is done he'll be killed on the spot where it's set. At least that's the line he's giving out. . . ."

We proceeded to Headquarters, where the horses were to be gathered before being driven to roundup. But we were still early, and the only one there was Ramon, who had been almost alone

since yesterday and seemed glad for the company. A man well into his sixties, with thick sunglasses, a blue visored cap, and prominent front teeth displayed in a nearly perpetual grin, despite his Mexican accent he seemed obscurely Chinese. Once reputedly the best hand at the o6, Ramon had followed a time-honored retirement plan: when he got too old to cowboy he became a cook.

Ramon's kitchen, a two-wheeled trailer hitched to a Ford camper, was a variation on the traditional chuckwagon. The trailer's back end dropped into a folding table, exposing a set of shelves filled with canned goods, pots, syrup, soap, and utensils. The trailer's bulk was a conglomerate of gunmetal gray boxes plus a small icebox, folding chairs, a plastic garbage can, cooking implements, and bottles of Clorox lashed to wire shelves along the side. The chuckwagon had been backed into one end of the Headquarters cook shed, a rectangular roof with low cement benches along two sides, to sit on or use as tables, and otherwise left open. In the center of the dirt floor lay a sunken live oak fire, with a coffee pot at one end over a separate bed of coals. Outside the shed stood a six foot wall of chopped live oak. The o6 was only one of Ramon's employers, and between roundups he hauled his movable feast to parties, dances, weddings — any occasion that wanted him. The occupation had its frustrations, such as when he prepared a full meal the previous night for cowboys stranded at a grass fire.

But his abilities were highly praised, and as he sat by his fold-out table reminiscing old times with Gordon, giggling and shoving potatoes through a device that knifed out French fries, curiosity edged into hunger.

Suddenly we heard a whoop, looked up, and saw Joel and a half-dozen other cowboys driving the o6 horses, the remuda, back from rock school. The roundup — or at least this second phase of it — was about to begin. On a ranch as large as the o6 the operations were necessarily handled in one area at a time, and the lower areas, easier of access, had already been worked on successive weekends with hired help from Alpine and Fort Davis. But on the distant mesas it simply wasn't practical to haul people, horses, food, bedding, and equipment for a weekend at a time, and a new headquarters had to be set up. For the next few days, therefore, the ranch would be run from the Number Nine Camp, the geological roof of the o6 and possibly Gordon's favorite spot in the world.

Horses and cowboys poured snorting and yelling into the corral. "Well, I gotta go sketch," said Gordon, grabbing his camera and pushing past me through the gates with our photographer Linda hot on his heels. The horses surged in a dizzying pack around the corral while the cowboys one by one roped their mounts and led them aside. An older cowboy named John advised the others while the

pack swirled en masse away from the ropes, and Gordon ducked in and out with his camera. "Look at John and the guy behind him," said Gordon excitedly. "Aren't they something?" One by one the horses were culled and put in a separate corral. A couple of cowboys were busy in a third corral shoeing the horses, driving nails through the hooves and breaking off the ends with dispatch, then all the cowboys lashed their saddles to the sides of a long horse trailer attached to a battered pickup.

From the o6 Headquarters the rest of the remuda would be driven to a corral several miles from the Number Nine Camp, ready for roundup to begin next dawn. Gordon was delighted at the timing: we would drive to the mesa slightly ahead of the remuda and watch it arrive in the false light of sundown. Barney had just arrived, and as we prepared to pile into Gordon's car, Chris Lacy came over and said that the pickup with the trailer full of saddles also needed to be driven: would I be willing? My experience with truck driving was confined to a few runs down the highway to the recycling center in a borrowed pickup full of beer cans, but I agreed. Knowing Linda had owned a truck for eight years, I asked her to come along and take the first stint at the wheel.

Gordon was so anxious to get beyond the remuda and watch it coming that he shot ahead and disappeared. Linda and I, opening gates and fording streams in our cumbersome rig, wondered if we'd taken the right road. We came upon Gordon taking pictures, and at my suggestion I took over the wheel. We bounced and careened up a hill to a windmill, got out and positioned ourselves next to a water tank so as not to spook the approaching horses. It was like a vision of our lost frontier, to watch the remuda flanked by three cowboys come galloping up the dusty valley, into our clicking cameras. Since the rig seemed easy enough to handle, Linda asked if it would be all right if she joined Gordon in his truck ahead, where she could get better pictures. She climbed onto his luggage rack, and rather like an African safari we proceeded.

The remuda continued down the long valley while the road turned to the right and began to climb gradually over rocks and pits, with Linda still clinging to the top. We reached some higher meadows, then the tracks wound and dipped, and I lost sight of Gordon. But there was only one road and I pressed on. How was it possible for Gordon, even in his excitement, to make such speed with someone on top? Linda must have gotten in, but how had I missed seeing it? As the road wound onward I felt less assured. I squinted to see tracks in the dust, could make out none, but I didn't want

to stop the truck and get further behind. Each time the road curved out of sight then back into view, I thought: Appear, Gordon, dammit, appear!

I continued along a gradual curve, past a windmill with a stock tank. At one point I noticed another road veering off, but it seemed even less used, still farther from the direction the remuda was traveling, and I wasn't tempted. I traversed a basin for several more miles, then spotted a tin shed and a tank. Surely that was the Number Nine Camp, and Gordon would be waiting. I reached the shed and found no car. Roads took off in three directions, none with detectable tracks. To proceed down any of them would be madness; the only sensible alternative was to return to Headquarters. If I got all the way back without running into Gordon, or someone else who knew what was happening, at least we would have a central meeting place, the ranch would know where the saddles were, and someone in authority could plan the next move.

I made a wide loop through the grass and started back in the last sun, down the basin, past the windmill, along the broad curve, over the meadows, and back down. Darkness was gradually folding in. The road reached a lower level, and I came to a closed gate. It was not a latch I recognized: had it stood open before? No matter; I threw the truck into neutral, opened the gate, and drove through. I turned the motor off, got out to close the gate behind me, and had to laugh: never having driven a truck with a trailer before, I'd left the trailer right in the middle of the gate. I got back in the truck and turned the key. The motor wouldn't start. By what evil instinct had I turned it off? I switched on the headlights, got out and inspected the road ahead for previous tracks. There were none. I got back in; the motor still wouldn't start. Was this possible? A car with someone on top had completely disappeared, then I'd driven out onto a mesa, returned precisely the same way, and was now on a strange road, halfway through a gate, in a stalled truck, in total darkness, with all the saddles for a roundup that was to begin at dawn. The poor o6: first grass fires, now this.

The only recourse was to remain calm and settle in for a long night. I had my own parka, someone else's parka, and Linda's sweater. I would be warm, safe, and my discomfort would be grimly mental. I stepped outside, examined the brilliant stars, listened to the ringing silence scored by a few distant crickets. Was that ringing the bass note of being or one's own inner ear? Or an approaching car? No, it was sheer absence. Such calm was perhaps the ranch's most luxurious possession, and I appreciated more viscerally the breadth of the o6. I considered a walk by starlight, but no, this was snake country and I lacked a flashlight. I got back in the cab and tried the motor again, to no effect. Had anyone realized I was missing? Would I be found at dawn? Would I be blamed for losing the saddles? I tried to think of anything I would have done differently and came up with nothing. It is at such moments one realizes the future is utterly opaque.

I tried the key again, and the roar of the motor almost frightened me. It had merely flooded. Grateful for a moment's activity, I continued through the gate, turned the motor back off and closed the gate behind me. At least I would be spared *that* humiliation. I crawled back in the cab and nestled in the parkas for an indefinite time. I became aware of shifting lights in the cab, then silence growled like an engine. I jumped from the cab. There were headlights at the gate and out of them walked Gordon and Joel.

I pulled the saddle truck out of the way, then squeezed into Gordon's truck, which turned out to be packed with his trio plus Joel and the other two cowboys who had driven the remuda. It took several tellings on each side, with one of the cowboys rendering it for another into Spanish, before we unraveled what had happened. Gordon, with Linda on top, had pulled off the road to take a picture, while I, eyes on the potholes, had driven by without seeing them. I continued to the Number Nine Camp with Gordon behind me. When they came to the lesser road I had rejected, Barney said that was the way to Number Nine, and they followed a tortuous road to the end of the mesa. By the time they realized their mistake, I had come and gone, night had fallen, and Gordon had missed seeing the remuda arrive in the last light. They concluded I had taken one of the three roads that led out from Number Nine and tried each in turn. The dust on the mesa is too fine to show treadmarks, so they kept looking for fresh cow chips that might show evidence of passage. Several times Barney saw the distant lights of Alpine and said, "There he is!" Joel thought one of the roads hadn't been adequately checked, and they tried it again. Their great fear was that I had continued past where they dared to search, down tracks that would have been lethal in a truck and trailer, and had met some obscure disaster. At last they ran out of roads, picked up the cowboys who had been waiting at the Number Nine Camp for a ride and started back. To their shock and relief they found me at a gate that Gordon had opened on the way up and that was, I then learned, Number Seven Pasture. So the upshot of the evening was that Gordon had missed his pictures, all had missed dinner, and Joel, having slept two hours a night for the last two, had missed sleep. By the time we reached the Nelsons it was crowding midnight, and tomorrow was scheduled to begin at three in the morning.

When we got up three hours later the glow of a late moonrise was just bulging on the horizon — like a distant grass fire, thought Gordon. The truck crawled in silence toward Headquarters as we tried to keep our eyes open for deer and javelina. The electric bulbs of the cook shed seemed garish as we pulled up, and when we got out the first sound I heard was a scream. "Eeeee-yah! Ah feel *wahld.*" Yes, I thought, this *is* Texas. But when we made our way through the rumpled cots that surrounded the cook shed, then stepped into the light, there were only a few cowboys slumped groggily on folding chairs. Ramon, his grin sheathed, was turning a pancake. Mark was still snug in his cot, and suddenly all the cowboys started yelling at him.

"Last call for alcohol!"

"No, Norman, don't pour that cold water on him! Last time you did that he got pneumonia for six weeks."

"Maybe he's drawin' a moustache with a eyebrow pencil."

Diane arrived with the news that a fresh outbreak of fire had been reported at one-thirty that morning. There was a stunned silence, then she went on to say that Chris had checked it out and

found it was a case of some motorist being alarmed by the dying coals. Ramon had prepared a full meal of French toast, bacon, pancakes, eggs to order, and a full pot of igneous coffee, cooked over a bed of coals lifted from the fire. I caused a small stir by ladling some of his special hot sauce over my pancakes, a move I thought might gain me a few points in the eyes of anyone who had blamed me for losing the saddles. *Chile macho*, at this hour? It was one of those *salsas* so hot you're likely to sneeze and throw your back out, and I slipped back for seconds. We blinked over more coffee while the cowboys folded their cots and loaded them into a large truck that would transport them to the Number Nine Camp.

We got into Gordon's truck along with Joel, Davy, and a couple more cowboys and bounced up the road we had just come back down hours earlier. The turns were nearly familiar. When we reached the saddle truck, Joel got out and drove behind us: the mix-up wouldn't delay roundup after all. "Gordon," said Mark, breaking the silence, "wasn't that paintin' you did of me the best thing you ever done?"

"Are you kidding?" said Gordon. "I had to pay a man fifty dollars to get rid of it."

"What did you call it?"

"*The Lone Star Kid.* You like that?"

"Yeah," said Mark without enthusiasm, "it's okay."

"Well at least it beats *Onion Face.*"

With his nasal drawl, not quite finishing his words, Mark reminded me of all those young Andalusians who dreamed of becoming cowboys. Mark was the kid they all wanted to be.

The turns I had driven with heightened awareness at sundown slid by comfortably through the dark. We passed the Number Nine Camp and reached the corralled horses in the aquarium light in which day seems to begin from no particular quarter. Arriving by long ascent, one had a sense of height, yet the land was flat and extensive, with the edge miles away and only the tops of distant ranges biting into the horizon. Cowboys piled out of trucks and warmed up by roping each other, laughing. One cowboy was thrown to the ground like a calf, with a loop around one foot and another around his chest as his friends pulled him in opposite directions. Then the cowboys entered the corral, and each roped his mount while the remuda skittered and revolved.

"Here comes that phony old sun," said Gordon, camera in hand as light broke over the horizon. Six cowboys just outside the corral were untracking — working their horses a bit before starting out

42 hangin' on

to reaccustom them to the cinch and decrease the likelihood of their bucking. Gordon was moving about quickly, trying to catch one of the cowboys in the first radiance. "Turn, Adulto, turn!" he yelled mostly to himself as he clicked in frustration. "Damn, last shot on the roll! Quick, Linda, hand me the other camera. . . ."

After the horses had been untracked, the cowboys loped off toward the extremities of the mesa, then Chris, Diane, and Steve loaded their mounts into a long horse trailer, which was needed near the mesa's end to haul back any calves that refused to be herded. Gordon, Linda, and I climbed with them into their two-seater pickup — and at last we were riding toward the actual roundup. Chris and Diane were to have been Joel and Barney's dinner guests the chaotic night of our arrival, but this was our first chance to talk with them.

Chris, in his early thirties and possessed of what *National Geographic* called "a grin wide as Texas," was young for a ranch manager. He had spent part of his childhood on the ranch and returned to take over after graduation from Texas Christian University. Inexperienced, a grandson of the owners, his command was predictably greeted with skepticism and potential hostility. But he learned so swiftly and threw himself so completely into ranching that he soon gained the ranch's respect as a manager and their personal devotion — a result I can believe after watching him supervise the fire line from the thick of the fray.

Diane's adaptation was still more radical, for she was a city girl from San Antonio and totally unfamiliar with ranch life when she met Chris at the university. She majored in art, played the piano, and was immersed in dancing, both classical and modern. "Dance," she said, "is my main background for ranching." Slim and petite, with long brown hair and delicate features, she too plunged wholly into the life, learned to herd cattle, to rope, to brand, and to hold her own with the best of hands. Ranching and raising children left time for little else, but she tried to maintain contact with the art world and was at the moment choreographing a *Salute to Broadway* for Sul Ross State University. "I still have the opening and closing numbers to do," she said, "and in my spare time at roundup I'll be dancing around the tent."

As sophisticated young managers, the Lacys are unusual in their devotion to traditional ranching, and the ranch is in turn unusual in allowing women to attend roundup. As wives of a full-time cowboy and the ranch manager, Barney and Diane have more secure positions. Gordon had explained to me the traditional code: a cowboy can say anything he dares about another cowboy's girlfriend, but a wife, by virtue of the marriage contract, is an extension of the cowboy himself and therefore off limits. Yet even wives have always been discouraged from attending roundup because the work is considered too physically demanding for most women. Those who attend the roundup without understanding it, or without helping out, only get in the way, cause an unnecessary burden on the food and, as objects of a chivalrous tradition, require special consideration. For women with families it is, in any case, difficult to get help, and they are needed at home if the ranch is to raise persons as well as cattle. A ranch marriage, said Gordon, is an equal partnership but with the roles sharply defined. The code is such that women themselves put pressure on each other not to intrude on men's terrain, and those who do lose status among the others.

The situation is different on the o6 and more progressive in terms of changing standards. The wives of the men in command happen to be good hands themselves and their presence contributes rather than interferes. The situation still has classic pitfalls. Barney reported an occasion in which she told Jack Pharriss she was going off toward the creek on private business, whereupon he dispatched Mark to help her get back a calf she'd gone after. Mark came loping up, wheeled and loped back faster than he arrived. Barney and Mark were both targets of much subsequent glee, and Barney was plotting suitable revenge.

Chris stopped the pickup a mile from the edge of the mesa, let out Steve's horse, then his horse Suture, who once gashed himself on the horse trailer, and Diane's horse Kung Fu, who kicks a lot.

44 hangin' on

When they were mounted, Gordon took a few pictures, and every time the shutter clicked, Steve's coil of rope chanced to be covering his face, he was scratching his nose, or his head was turned, all in a spontaneous pantomime that just happened to keep his features from being recorded. Then they were off to join the roundup.

Here and there, singly and in far groups, we could see moving dots that the binoculars resolved into cowboys. The sun was brilliant, the air crisp and somehow charged. Suddenly Chris reappeared driving a rebellious bull calf that kept veering off in another direction. When the calf passed the horse trailer Chris roped him. The calf dug his legs in like a recalcitrant hound, then darted around the side of the trailer, flaring his nostrils and breathing heavily. Gordon grabbed the tail, and pulling both ends they harassed him to the back of the trailer, where he lay down. Chris asked Gordon to tail him up. Gordon, who seemed as practised as any of the cowboys, grabbed the tail with an upward twist that brought him to his feet, while Chris passed the rope around one of the posts of the trailer and pulled. Balking and snorting, the calf stumbled inside, and Gordon slammed the gate.

Calves that refused to herd were the exception, but they showed the power and will of an animal still only a fraction of its eventual size. There is a saying that if you have all your fingers you don't know how to rope, and I could see that the brute force at the end of a line was far greater than a man's and could only be overcome by ingenuity. Any lapse of attention could be risky, and particularly deadly was the dally, the rope coiled around the saddle horn. A finger caught in the slack might go its own way, and ten-fingered cowboys like Chris did well to confound the saying.

Chris rode off to rejoin the roundup, and Gordon turned the pickup around so we could inch forward and watch. Beginning from the edge of the mesa, cowboys were gradually working their way toward the corrals. The cattle, seemingly unaware any of this concerned them, merely moved away from the cowboys. The cowboys pressed the gathering clusters to keep the animals from straying or stopping to graze, but were careful not to crowd them or in any way cause them to turn aside. In the distance we could see an occasional cowboy galloping after a stray. It is in the nature of cowboys to

hangin' on **45**

enjoy chasing cattle, in the nature of bosses to want the animals walked and kept calm, and any cowboy caught provoking a cow took his chances. But a certain number inevitably strayed from the groups, and when the inevitable happened the cowboys gave glorious chase.

Groups of men were approaching on all sides now, surrounding the thickening groups of cattle, the animals still unmindful they were headed to a focal point in a psychological net slowly pulled tight. Watching the raw strength of the animals, the control of the men, and the clean expanse of grass, it was easy to understand the continuing fascination of such a scene for an artist like Gordon. "That's the life," he said, "that's the greatest thing in the world, to ride through this open country doing that. If we had a few more days, I'd be out there with them. And when I paint them, it's really myself I'm painting." I could see that his devotion to being purely an artist was bought at some cost, for at the moment he would love to be a real rather than a vicarious cowboy. And even the observer could see that in the tension between animal momentum and human strategy was something elemental, resonant with more than the mere act of gathering. No matter how tired one might be of such scenes in movies, or the cowboy legend itself, it was hard not to be excited by the breathing

46 hangin' on

presence of the herd, or the pageantry of these men with their brilliant colors and difficult skills, moving across the tawny landscape like tropical birds.

By the time we reached the pens, the herd was a single tight roaring mass being driven into an area fenced on two sides and giving way to the pens. Cowboys in the distance were still galloping after strays. Steve rode in with a calf the size of a German shepherd draped in front of his saddle, over the horse's neck. It seemed complicated enough to keep the horse calm, the calf from falling off, and remain mounted himself, but he remembered to crook his neck at an impossible angle to put the brim of his hat between his face and Gordon's distant camera. A horse wandered back unmounted, then a cowboy appeared with a calf on a lead. "How about *Walking the Dogie!*" suggested Gordon.

The gates were opened and the cattle funneled in. The pens became a crush of bellowing flesh with cowboys, on foot now, whooping and whistling among cattle clamoring in flat disgusted tones every vowel from ah to ooh. Out of this knotted chaos the cattle were being cut into separate pens, cows into one, yearlings in another, calves born since last spring's roundup in a third. Chris cautioned us to watch by the post; anyone in the open might spook the cattle and make them more unmanageable still.

48 hangin' on

A branding iron stand was set up near the pen holding the youngest calves, with a hose running to a butane tank in the back of a pickup. Gordon said he had never seen two stands alike and was planning one day to make drawings of all the ones he had seen. This one featured a thick metal tube with a head-like vent at one end and a framework of pipes that resembled legs, and looked oddly like a futuristic rocking horse. An open rectangle in the flank gave way to the fire. Four irons with the o6 brand were being heated until they glowed scarlet, while heat rose above them in waves and sparks flew out, lit on the dry grass, and had to be stamped out.

Cowboys in pairs wrestled the calves to the ground, a man at each end, pinning them with their arms, their legs, and their torsos. Gordon plunged into the thick of it, helping to hold the rebellious calves while Diane took one of the branding irons from the stand and pressed it into the animal's hindquarters. The flesh sizzled, the hide briefly flared, and smoke curled sharp with the smell of burning hair. A cowboy with a large hypodermic needle gave the animal a quick shot. Another grabbed the testicles and cut them swiftly. Another cut the horns, then untwisted them by the roots with a hollow instrument resembling a socket wrench. Another took a knife and made a slit on the underside of the left ear. Then a disinfectant that looked like clear glue was slapped on with a wide

brush, and the calf was released.

The maneuvers followed in quick succession, but throughout, the animals thrashed and struggled, filling the pen with their bellowing and bleating. Their eyes, usually soft and dark, rolled back to show the bluish and viscous whites, giving their bland faces a look of terror. Calves waiting their turn stood huddled and bawling at the far end of the corral, and at one point I noted equal groups of animals cowering in all four corners. One calf was so young it was still trailing part of its umbilical cord. The one that yelled the loudest seemed dizzy afterward, staggering and stumbling to regain its balance. Others were quiet and impassive, and perhaps had gone into shock. Blood glittered from the sides of animals' heads, ran down their legs, and splashed more darkly onto denim, faces, and human hands. The smell of burning hair became nauseous, and Diane, former art student and present choreographer, raised her kerchief over her nose and mouth and pressed on. Mark was nowhere to be seen. One little calf in a corner lay collapsed and shaking; Jack Pharriss went over and patted it gently and helped it to its feet.

With three or four calves held down at a time by pairs of cowboys while the others circled quickly to perform their operations, it took an hour and a half to work through the entire pen. The

ordeal may have lasted no more than a minute for each calf, though who knows how it reckoned in the animal's eternal present. After the last calf had been processed, a pickup hauling a metal tank pulled up and the cowboys hosed all the cattle with repellent that brought back memories of the town where I grew up, of elms full of the chemical sweetness of DDT.

Was all of this really necessary? Branding, of course, was for identification, and so were the slits in the ears, for the brand was often obscured by winter coats, or hard to read from a distance. Each ranch had its own cuts, and the cow when approached would spread its ears and show them clearly. Castration controlled the breeding. Dehorning made steers easier to deal with, but more importantly, it kept them from goring and bruising each other, particularly in the eye, when they were herded into trucks and shipped to feedlots. Inoculation prevented blackleg; spraying prevented screw worm. If any of these moves bothered the cowboys, by now they were used to it, and they lost no face with displays of tenderness. The mood of the pens was businesslike and even humorous, though not at the animals' expense. The younger the animal, said Gordon, the less developed the nervous system and the less they feel. Perhaps, but for the ranch it was simply the way of doing business.

By mid-afternoon the cattle were ready to be turned out of the pens, and the cows and calves

52 hangin' on

were herded slowly back to the pasture they came from. They moved more deliberately now, bellowing little, and the cowboys walked them patiently, letting them get over their trauma, letting mothers find their calves by sniffing their breath. Calves would remain with other cows until their mother showed up, and any cow would run off a predator that threatened a stray calf. This was a far different herd from the brawling and spirited mob that had arrived a few hours earlier.

These scenes of gathering and branding would be repeated over and over during the next three weeks as cowboys moved from pasture to pasture, moving camp to different parts of the mesa, into remote corners of the ranch. I asked Gordon whether he ever painted this aspect of ranching. Branding, he said, had been done and redone until every conceivable aspect had become a cliché. As for the rest . . . When I thought of living room walls the thought hardly needed completing.

Basins of soap and water were set out by the chuckwagon, then the meal Ramon had been preparing during the branding was strung out along the coals: a buffet of beef ribs, green beans, rice, beef stew, refritos, and a huge Dutch oven bearing the largest peach cobbler I have seen. All except the cobbler had rich, dark flavors, heavily peppered and spiced. I thought of the animals that provided the ribs and the beef in the stew, suffering the same shocks I had just witnessed. But the vicarious

ordeal had left me ironically drained, and I ate with gusto. I finished the food as it was, then returned for seconds on the rice, heaped it with *chile macho* and went out in a blaze of glory.

After lunch the cowboys, active since before dawn, sat in small groups talking, stretched out with their hats over their faces, or crawled under the pickups for a catnap in the shade. But the day was not over, for the yearlings still had to be weaned by being driven to a new pasture, and the remuda had to be back at the Number Nine Camp to be ready to begin work next day. Chris asked me to drive the pickup with this morning's rebellious calf to Number Nine Camp, and I was glad that my ability to find it had not gone unnoticed.

We arrived ahead of the remuda and inspected the cabin. It was filled with the cots we had watched being loaded after breakfast at Headquarters, some inside, others on the porch in a kind of open dormitory. It was hot, I still felt empty from so many sensations and little sleep, and wandered about listening to meadowlarks call from rock to rock in the sun. The remuda poured in, and we gathered by the corral to watch. As I stood chatting with Diane, Gordon came over and suggested something cool to drink.

Gordon, Diane, Steve, Joel, Linda, and I converged at the tailgate. Steve reached avidly for the Shasta Colas, popped them open and thrust them icy and foaming into our hands. "Thanks," said Diane, handing hers back, "but I'm on a diet because of the show at Sul Ross."

"Then have a Tab," replied Steve with such authority that she could only comply.

Conversation led to a round of toasts. To the roundup. To no more grass fires. To the visitors. To the hosts. To Diane's dances. To Gordon's paintings. To Linda's photographs. To my text.

As we neared the bottom of the cans, Steve reached into the cooler, grabbed a round of Gatorade and dealt them out. Diane accepted hers without complaint. Linda sprayed some on herself.

"Here, let me wipe it off. Soon as I can pry my kerchief apart," said Steve, struggling as if with a glued knot. With that we were off on enough stories to insult every minority group we might have

54 hangin' on

belonged to, led by Steve with the gestures and timing of an accomplished comedian. Leading to another round. Were we really leaving in the morning? To torn plane tickets!

Gordon suddenly remembered that in our fascination with roundup we hadn't seen any of the canyons that plunged off the mesa. Diane said she had lived nine years on the ranch without seeing all of them herself. On, then, to Hatch Canyon!

We piled into Gordon's cantina and roared off on another of the roads that led from Number Nine Camp, bouncing and laughing in bursts of foam. Was it the camaraderie, or were we rashly mixing our drinks? We got out at a small reservoir, balanced single file along the rim, then started down the slope beneath it. We stumbled garrulously around Spanish bayonets, over loose rocks in a skirmish of voices. "I once won a contest for throwing a cow chip farther than anyone else," proclaimed Gordon.

"I knew you were the most award-winning CAA artist," I said, "but . . ."

"Yeah, by a hundred and fifty yards."

"I wish I was an eagle," said Steve. "Course I'd have to fly outa Texas where the goat herders couldn't shoot me."

Ahead we could see fragments of a drop-off, where the dark crumbling foreground gave way to far drifts of sable. At the edge stood a precarious finger of basalt like the chimney of a burned house. Steve, sprinting ahead, clambered to the top, threw his arms out with a Bubble Up can in one hand and yelled, "Hey, everybody, take my picture!" Through our very fog we were stunned. Was this suppressed desire? A suicide? Were we to take his image and launch him into the brink?

We clicked obediently, Steve scrambled back down, and we filed thoughtfully around the rock. We gazed through an arch that framed the lower darkness, then paused in an Indian cave that seemed almost untouched, waxing profound about the Past and how few had come this way Since. The volcanic walls began to close in. We made our way through a slot with standing pools and came to a sheer drop. We gazed into pale nothingness. Canyon wrens sang their crystalline scales and we croaked back. We sacrificed virgin rocks to the abyss. Joel confessed that as an avid hunter he would never shoot his favorite duck, the bufflehead. Gordon presumably was balancing a headful of pictures. Linda was beginning to look like my lost cousin Jean. "We better get outa here," muttered Gordon, "before we get too dark."

I looked back on grass fires, conversations, the lost truck, the roundup, the branding. Had it been only three days? Did people on the ranch always live this intensely? Was such a life still possible? And as the last light fled the 06, burnishing rimrock and seeding the fields with night, I felt that the question I'd put to Gordon had been fully answered. This, somehow, was how art got started.

56 hangin' on

The Paintings

THE BUCKAROOS *Oil 48 x 60 inches 1979*

10 A.M. AND DONE A DAY'S WORK   *Opaque Watercolor*   *23 x 28 inches*   *CAA Gold Medal for Watercolor 1975*

EYEING THE CATCH HAND   *Opaque Watercolor   24 x 36 inches   CAA Gold Medal for Other Media 1979*

THE HAPPY HOUR   *Oil   35½ x 36 inches   CAA Memorial Award 1979*

MOONLIGHTING   *Opaque Watercolor   24 x 36 inches   1979*

SATURDAY NIGHT WHISKEY: A BUNCH OF SUNDAY MORNING HURT   *Opaque Watercolor   15¼ x 20¼ inches*
CAA Best of Show and Gold Medal for Other Media 1978

SPECIAL DELIVERY   *Opaque Watercolor   19 x 23¼ inches   1979*

A SURE ENOUGH GOOD HAND   *Opaque Watercolor   20½ x 34 inches   CAA Silver Medal for Other Media 1976*

ABEL OF THE CHILICOTE   *Opaque Watercolor   25 x 34 inches   CAA Best of Show and Gold Medal for Other Media 1977*

FRANK: PORTRAIT OF A COWBOY *Opaque Watercolor* *19 x 22⅜ inches* *1979*

END OF THE DAY   *Oil   36 x 48 inches   1976*

KEITH   *Opaque Watercolor   16½ x 34½ inches   1977*

SUNUP   *Opaque Watercolor   19 x 25 inches   1979*

MY DRINKING BUDDY FROM THE CRYSTAL BAR   *Opaque Watercolor   24½ x 25 inches   1979*

AMERICAN PAINT *Oil   20 x 30 inches   1974*

CUTTING OUT A TOUGH CUSTOMER *Opaque Watercolor 28½ x 23⅝ inches*
Western Art Associates Purchase Award, Phoenix Art Museum 1977

AFTER THE RAIN *Opaque Watercolor* *13½ x 24 inches* 1975

WEASEL   *Opaque Watercolor   17½ x 17½ inches   1975*

LARRY   *Opaque Watercolor   12 x 16 inches   1974*

THE SUNSHINE KID   *Opaque Watercolor   16⅞ x 18¾ inches   1979*

OLD BONES AND BAD EYES   *Opaque Watercolor   13⅛ x 16½ inches   1977*

BEFORE THE SUN GETS WARM   *Opaque Watercolor   24 x 31 inches   1978*

COWBOY HEAVEN: A WARM TENT, A CUP OF COFFEE, AND A CIGARETTE *Oil   36 x 42½ inches   1980*

LITTLE BIT DOING BIG STUFF   *Opaque Watercolor   22¾ x 34¼ inches   1978*

LIGHTING UP *Opaque Watercolor 13½ x 26 inches 1976*

THE VAQUERO *Pastel 12 x 16 inches 1977*

THE TOBACCO KID *Opaque Watercolor 15⅝ x 19¾ inches 1979*

THE SKEPTIC   *Opaque Watercolor   16⅛ x 23 inches   1979*

THE WINTERING CAP   *Opaque Watercolor   15 x 19 inches   1978*

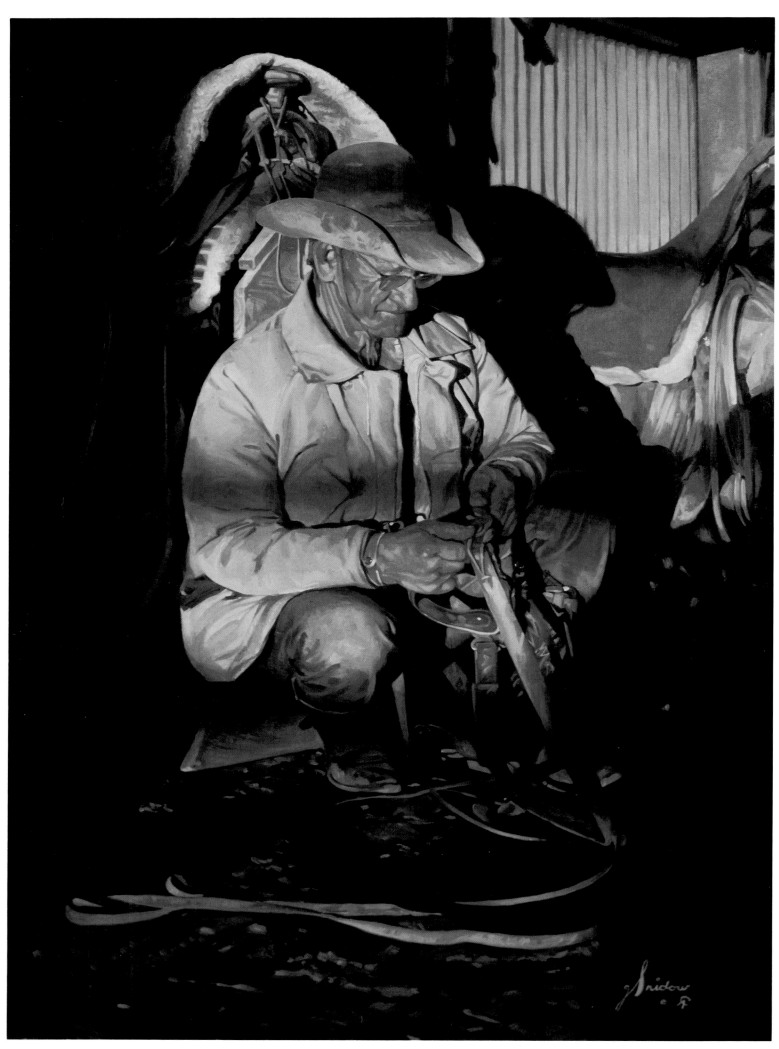

A REMNANT OF ANOTHER TIME   *Oil   36 x 48 inches   CAA Memorial Award 1978*

A DUSTY MORN *Oil   22½ x 30 inches   1974*

THE DREAMER   *Opaque Watercolor and Colored Pencil   25½ x 17½ inches   CAA Gold Medal for Other Media 1975*

THE LITTLEST STRAGGLER   *Oil   24 x 36 inches   1978*

COLORADO COOLADE   *Opaque Watercolor*   *14½ x 25 inches*   *1977*

DAYBREAK AT THE DIAMOND A *Oil 27 x 40 inches 1976*

O'MISERY *Opaque Watercolor 24 x 36 inches 1980*

LOOKING FOR THE PIEBALD MARE   *Opaque Watercolor   24 x 36 inches   1979*

NUMBER NINE CAMP   *Opaque Watercolor   28¼ x 25¾ inches   1978*

THAT SUCKER'S GONNA BUCK, SURE AS HELL   *Opaque Watercolor   25 x 36 inches   1980*

Destination

I F YOU WERE GOING TO PAINT A COWBOY ABOUT TO RIDE A SKITTISH HORSE, THE MOST obvious way would be to show the cowboy actually trying to mount the horse, to get some action. You would at least have the horse and cowboy face to face, and you certainly wouldn't put the cowboy's back to the viewer. But when I hit upon the way to do *That Sucker's Gonna Buck, Sure As Hell*, I decided to show it through postures. The horse has one ear forward, one ear back, and his eyes are rolled back to show a bit of white. He doesn't know himself what he's going to do next. You don't see the cowboy's face except for a bit of profile, or anything of the eyes except for the rim of his glasses. What you get is the cowboy from the back with his arms crossed and his torso bent slightly one way and his head the other, as if he's studying the horse. There's light on the cowboy's hand and on the rein that's the physical tension between them. The real contact is eye to eye, but only one eye is shown and it's the body positions that say it."

"To keep the strong silhouettes, I made the setting simple as possible, and I didn't want anything in the background to compete or clutter it up. But I didn't want the horizon cutting across in a straight line either. So I broke it up with a bit of rimrock on one side and some distant trees on the other, both caught in a bit of light. The horizon is really a soft line, which you need with a sky as flat as that. The sky is almost white, and almost looks unpainted, but it's actually graded from warm to cool while keeping the same values. Unless you have a sharp eye you can't tell, but there are six colors going on in that sky. And I've used the same low light to bring out the texture of the grass in the foreground. Of course all this is only what the artist works from. What's important for the viewer is how it hits him."

Gordon, standing next to his painting in a white shirt, tie, and beige suit, minus his cowboy hat, looked somehow leaner and sleeker than he did on the 06 and less in his element. Three bars dispensed free drinks, a piano trio played upbeat cocktail music on stage, and under a sprawling chandelier, dead center, stood a buffet table full of hot hors d'oeuvres arrayed around two ice sculptures: the head of a horse and the head of a steer. The icy, metallic smell of the air conditioning gradually warmed with the perfumes and scents of humanity as groups entered the room through security guards and a bower of young bamboo, picked up their libations and started the rounds of the walls. We were in the Emerald Room of the Shamrock Hilton in Houston, and the cocktail party that launched the fifth annual Western Heritage Sale had just thrown open the gates.

Along the walls of the great salon were paintings and bronzes, beneath which hung small cardboard boxes with slits for dropping intent-to-purchase slips. Gordon was one of five artists who had met at intervals during the year to plan the event and decide which artists should be invited. With him for the weekend were Sue, his daughter Laurie, his son Steve, and several friends from Ruidoso: clearly he was here to enjoy himself as well as sell paintings. The music stopped; former Texas governor John Connally bounded to the stage and announced that the crowd would be allowed an hour and a half to view the art. Then the boxes would be collected and a name drawn from each allowing that person to purchase the work. "If you don't get to buy your favorite," he warned, "you'll still have time to drop your name in another box, so pay attention." I asked Gordon whether these events made him nervous.

"I've been working on this one all year, so it's not exactly like coming in cold. I've had great experiences at sales, and terrible ones, and I know what to hope for and what to dread. But it's hard not to have butterflies with your soul up there on the wall."

Tonight's advice on the program, Dress Casual, was variously interpreted, with women in pants suits and full gowns, men in coats and ties and jeans, separately and in combination. Artists belonging to the CAA sported large silver and brass official buckles. Evoking the Western mood was a lady in a red square-dance dress with white polka dots, a white bow with red polka dots, alligator boots, shiny lipstick, rouge, hair in fifties fluff, and Stetson. Cameras from KPRC-TV, Houston, panned the proceedings. While Gordon made his way through the crowd greeting friends and enthusiasts, I stood by his paintings — *That Sucker* and a smaller, single standing figure called *The Apprentice* — to catch the comments. The crowd grew animated on free drinks, ran their voices together and sometimes swept me downstream, but I retrieved a few:

"Isn't this contemporary! Look at the glasses on that cowboy . . ."

"I think this work could be very important."

"*The Apprentice* is my favorite but I do have one picky criticism. I wish he'd used a silver belt instead of a leather one."

"Seems like we're in the most congested corner. Shall we move on?"

An elderly man excitedly dragged another over by the arm. "Look at this, J.R. The way this horse has one ear one way, one the other and his eye rolled back. It's called *That Sucker's Gonna Buck, Sure As Hell.* And look how the guy with the glasses is studying him — you can just tell those two are psyching each other out. That cowboy may ride him, but he's sure gonna get worked. That's what I love about Western art — if you've actually done the stuff in the painting, it sure means a lot."

"This stuff is too photographic. Shall we proceed?"

"Sure is a wild look to that horse. What's it called, Iris?"

Iris bent over, squinting. "*That Sucker's Gonna Buck Him Off.*"

"First time I've seen a gouache going for that much. But this one may be worth it."

"There's Big John. Wanna say hello?"

"My God, this corner's crowded. Are we going the wrong way?"

"Know what this one's called, dear? *That Sucker's Gonna . . .*"

"Give me my rum and Coke."

"I've seen them all twice now, and this is the *one.*"

Connally returned to the stage and began to draw names out of boxes, while cheers from winning parties echoed around the room. I approached the hors d'oeuvre table for sustenance and found the only items left were some mysterious objects in tempura batter, which burst mid-bite into so vicious a strain of jalapeños they brought back tearful memories of *chile macho* on the o6. Connally drew the winning slip for Number 169, *That Sucker's Gonna Buck, Sure As Hell*, and it fell to a couple that had tried to buy one of Gordon's paintings at the last show in Phoenix, hadn't been picked, and were now beaming with delight. But this sale, for all its spice, was itself the merest hors d'oeuvre.

The next evening we followed a red carpet outside the hotel, past the entrance to Trader Vic's and into a side door. We crossed a vestibule of decorator plants and security guards and reached a blue carpet. We threaded a long hall with more plants on one side and stalls with quarter horses on the other; lithe, delicate, and curried to the last gleam. Fanciers paused to size them up and to study signs giving the ranch, lineage, and statistics. The blue carpet reached astroturf at a large room with three bars and a country-western band at one end, more quarter horses along the far wall, and a partition with rows of cattle in the middle. These were Santa Gertrudis, the first purely American breed of cattle, developed on the King Ranch in Texas. A deep brown so sleeked that light glinted from their hides, their rumps proudly branded as if signed by the artist, they were so thick and low slung it seemed miraculous they could even stand. When they did roll onto the hay, the tenders slapped their hindquarters and they drew themselves grudgingly up.

On the remaining wall, occupying the least space and commanding the most attention, were twenty-five works of art. Like the twenty-five horses and twenty-five cattle, they were to be auctioned off, and the committee had narrowed the field to the most qualified, to be represented by one work apiece. Artists withheld their best work for this event, and those with a single work to show offered it here. Gordon was represented by an oil showing a cowboy seated on a bedroll inside his tent, relaxing with coffee and a cigarette, but the painting's real subject was a golden radiance that spread through the canvas to illumine the simple objects, and particularly the cowboy's thoughtful face.

Again we had an hour and a half to look and drink, but this time there was no hope of holding ground in front of a painting. The program demanded Black Tie, and as usual at such events the women appeared in every cut and color of gown. But this time the men were not merely a uniform shadow for displaying the women, but occasionally burst forth in their own right with tuxes of beige, turquoise, and purple, with trousers tucked into cowboy boots, and feathered Stetsons. Cameras from NBC-TV panned from cows to tuxedos. At last the band left off playing "Waltz Across Texas," an electric guitar gave the horn call that announces a race, and the doors opened to the Grand Ballroom.

We poured into a vista of round tables gleaming with glass, silver, snowy linen, and stands with numbers corresponding to numbers on our name tags. Mirror stripping on the far walls and a paneled ceiling with crystal hemispheres of light magnified the brilliance. In the center of one wall stood a speakers' platform, and below it but above table height an iron pen entered on one side, passed in front of the stand and exited on the other. I located Table Thirty-five and was joined by an array of dinner companions. We exchanged names and places of origin, then someone asked the gentleman from Tahoe his occupation.

"I have gold mines," he replied. When our eyebrows quivered, he added, "In fact, I have a small sample of our product with me." He reached into his pocket, produced an ingot the size of a hotel soap and passed it around. It was *heavy.*

"How much is it worth?" inquired the lady to my right.

"$8,300 this morning."

The young Houston couple was asked their own occupation, and the man replied that he was a beginning sculptor, had hopes of being invited to show at a future Heritage Sale, and in fact his first one-man show was opening in Joske's parking lot tomorrow. "I have a sample of my work outside in the trunk of the car, if anybody's interested. . . ."

The couple to my right had a local art gallery. "Do you handle any of the artists in the show?" I asked.

"Not directly," the lady replied, "but often on the secondary market, when people want to sell what they've bought here or elsewhere."

"Ladies and gentlemen," announced John Connally from the speakers' stand, "someone has lost a gold cuff link in the shape of a horse's head." Suddenly a great oversized easel of white gladiolas behind the speakers' stand swooped forward, narrowly missing Connally, and sank, never to reappear. Connally introduced his Heritage co-sponsors, ranchers Louis Pearce and Joe Marchman, then Governor Clements and his wife, and the auction began.

While Connally praised the breeding, the ranch, and the rancher, a quarter horse was led in from one side of the pen and posed in front of the speakers' stand. An auctioneer next to Connally gabbled faster than the speed of hearing while assistants in tan tuxedos and straw cowboy hats with feathered medallions ranged through the audience, drummed up and caught the bids and yelled them back upstage. Faster than one could follow it the horse was sold and led out the right, a Santa Gertrudis bull entered from the left and the process began again. When the first painting was brought in, to Connally's lavish praise, images of it flashed overhead on two screens in the room's far corners, and the work itself was paraded high around the speakers' stand. The auctioneers gave it the same treatment. As each sale was completed, a third screen showed the projected lot number, name of purchaser, and sale price, penciled on a list by the shadow of a hand.

Drinks arrived, and more drinks, while animals and artworks were auctioned off: horses so sleek they seemed synthetic, bulls like breathing mahogany, paintings shown once in the flesh and twice on the wall. We savaged the hors d'oeuvre tray. The aspiring sculptor struck up a very interested conversation with the gallery lady across from me. Drinks kept arriving, food didn't, voices bellowed, and prices rose. Images of animals brought higher prices than live ones. Last year's highest sale had been $73,000, a world record for Western art, and I asked the gallery lady whether anything tonight might top $100,000. "At least three of them," she answered crisply. Listening to the auctioneer jabbering in a kind of continual drumroll one realized that the numbers sang through clearly and the rest didn't matter. The competitive hysteria from the floor and the auctioneer raving that the price wasn't enough contrasted oddly with the calm, balanced, wish-fulfilling visions on the two screens. Still odder was the third screen, the shadowed hand on the wall, calmly writing figures with an eerie suggestion of Belshazzar's feast: you are weighed in the balance and found short.

At last Gordon's painting was brought out. Connally praised Snidow's work, and this painting in particular, for their contemporary values, their strong composition, their masterful handling of light, the artist's magnificent future; then the bidding began. In such mayhem it was impossible to see who was shouting the numbers, and I hadn't spotted Gordon himself since the cocktail hour, but the final figure was $39,000 — $2,000 higher than his previous top sale.

By the time the salad arrived, two and a half hours after the first sit-down drinks, world records had been broken and rebroken. The gallery owner was correct in her prediction, and we debated whether the art market was currently so explosive because investors didn't trust anything that wasn't one of a kind. By the time we tore into our steak and lobster tail combo, the highest selling painting — a Mexican street scene and therefore not actually cowboy art — had gone for $170,000, more than double last year's record. The shadowed hand recorded the sum in blue pencil. Connally had the buyer stand up for applause, and also the bidder, whose losing offer was itself a world record when he made it.

"What you have to realize," said Gordon when it was all over, "is that the Western Heritage is only one aspect of the sale of Western art. The sale in Phoenix is a calm museum show, with fixed prices and a judged competition, open only to members of the CAA. The sale in Houston is unbridled free enterprise, where cowboy artists show along with those painting other aspects of the West, and those who can pay the highest prices show up. Phoenix and Houston are probably the most important annual events in cowboy art — and the extremes. There are also gallery auctions, private sales, commissions, the annual National Academy of Western Artists show at the Cowboy Hall — all kinds of ways cowboy art reaches the public. The Heritage Sale is only the wildest."

Seeing Gordon in his kitchen in Ruidoso, then on the o6, then in Houston, one realizes how many overlapping, even contradictory worlds a successful Western artist must inhabit. One imagines a painter sweating over his work in a studio, hauling it to a gallery and somehow getting paid, and there the image stops. But for Gordon a painting is born on a ranch, among his subjects, in a moment when what he sees and what he conceives come together in an imagined composition. At home, slowly and privately, the vision takes shape. Completed, it may go to Phoenix or Houston, to a chosen gallery, to a private collector, to the person who commissioned it. The act of painting reaches back to a moment of intuition face to face with its content and reaches ahead to its entry in the world. To function as a successful artist, Gordon must be able to make his way with cowboys, with art dealers, with admirers and collectors, with his fellow artists, to feel at home amid the sweat and dust of the o6 and the glitter of Houston — and still produce.

Once Gordon's paintings have left his hands, he may never learn their fate. Even if he meets the original buyer, the painting may change hands, be traded or sold, until there is no tracing it. Or it may suffer a more unexpected fate, such as the commission he painted for Coors that wound up hanging at the Grand Palais in Paris. Reproduced, his pictures find their way into bars, homes, dormitories, doctors' offices, magazines, museum shops, and even come full circle to hang on the walls of cowboys. To keep track of his career, Gordon must take pictures of his paintings before they leave his hands. When I told a friend I was writing a book on Gordon Snidow, my friend replied he'd never heard of him. When I showed him a poster by way of explanation, he exclaimed, "That's *Saturday Night Whiskey!*"

Gordon has stated that when he paints the cowboy, he is really painting himself. If so, he has magnified and extended that self through every sensibility that has come to identify with it. His works disperse, travel, live a life of their own even as they shrink for him to a box of transparencies. By remaining faithful to a tradition even as it changes, he is leaving us the look and feel of a way of life that will change once again. And by finding the enduring humanity beyond that change, he has transformed himself into a still more treasured spokesman: an artist of the people.

DESIGNED BY MARK SANDERS
COMPOSED IN PHOTOTYPE TRUMP
WITH DISPLAY LINES IN GOUDY CATALOGUE
PRINTED AT NORTHLAND PRESS

BOUND BY ROSWELL BOOKBINDING